LIVING FOR THE WEEKEND

The Winding Road Towards Balancing

Career Work and Spiritual Life

KEVIN HUNTER

WARRIOR
OF LIGHT
PRESS

Warrior of Light Press
www.kevin-hunter.com

Body, Mind & Spirit/Spiritualism
Inspiration & Personal Growth

Dedication

This is for my fellow hardworking people in the world, the working class, the ones with dreams of fulfilling your life purpose, the ones looking to do work that brings you and others joy.

CHAPTERS

THE MANIFESTATION AND ABUNDANCE

BONUS SECTION

AUTHOR'S NOTE

Thank you to those who shared their stories, concerns, and frustrations about their work lives over the years. This inspired *Living for the Weekend* to come to fruition. It's a topic my Spirit team had wanted to work with me to cover because of the detrimental impact that work can have on the well-being state of the planet. It's no surprise that much of ones life tends to revolve around work. Sometimes that can overpower, take you over, and then pull you under to the point that you've lost that spark and life force you were born with.

Living for the Weekend is designed to empower you to incorporate balance and understanding while helping you also transform your views about work and your life in general. This is infused with practical messages and divine guidance that my Spirit team has taught and shared with me revolving around the general areas of work, career, spirituality, and abundance. The main goal is to fine-tune your body, mind and soul. You are a Divine communicator capable of receiving messages and guidance from Heaven, as all souls are regardless if they believe in that or not.

The messages, guidance, information, and topics included in this book are areas that my Spirit team has guided me to discuss. My team makes up God and the Holy Spirit, as well as a team of guides, angels, and sometimes Archangels and Saints. I am merely the liaison or messenger in delivering and interpreting the intentions of what they wish to communicate.

Born with dominating Clairaudience and Claircognizance, with varying degrees of Clairsentience and Clairvoyance, my Spirit team comprises some hard truth telling Wise Ones from the other side, including Saint Nathaniel, who can be brutal in his truthful forcefulness. He cuts right to the heart of humanity without apology. I have learned quite a bit from him while adopting his ideology, which is Heaven's philosophy as a whole.

If I use the word "He" when pertaining to God, this does not mean that I am advocating that he is a male. Replace the word with one you are comfortable using to identify God for you to be. If the word, "God" makes you uncomfortable, then substitute it with one you're more familiar with such as light, energy, force, etc. This goes for any gender I use as examples. When I use the phrase, *Spirit Team*, I am referring to a team of *Guides and Angels*.

One of the purposes of my work is to empower, enlighten, as well as entertain. It's to help you improve yourself, your soul, your life and humanity as a result. It does not matter if you are a beginner or well versed in the subject matter. There may be something that reminds you of something you already know or something that you were unaware of. We all have much to share with one another, as we are all one in the end.

~ Kevin Hunter

LIVING FOR THE WEEKEND

CHAPTER ONE

The Modern Day Work World

I've been conducting years of research and pouring through endless data surrounding the current work environment state. This has included interviewing countless numbers of people, listening to their work lifestyle stories, questions, and struggles. All of this has revealed something disheartening that shouldn't be too surprising for those in the work force. The existing work arena has been long overdue for a major renovation. The way it's designed today is rapidly crushing and killing the well-being of millions of human souls. It's grown exceedingly out of control since the corporate worlds rose to prominence.

Having been out in the field in the workforce for decades and communicating with other professionals over the years about it has revealed some interesting revelations. The top two areas of concern I receive the most questions from people on surround work and love life. At this point, work and career related concerns have been coming in with stronger force over love related worries. Part of this can be because many people have been finding it more difficult to focus on love relationships when their work life is experiencing some form of chaos or disarray.

Until ones dreams are realized it can be challenging to focus on a love relationship, yet at the same time having a strong love partnership can in fact breathe life into career and work related endeavors. This is because people need some kind of moral support, including the most independent put together person. This independent person may not need as much coaching or support, but they can still use some love essence being breathed into their soul from another. What better champion to have in your life than a steady loyal love partner. Love relationships are a two way street, so if both partners are not giving each other that mutual support, then this will have a negative effect on other aspects of your life, including the work and career side of your existence.

The world has forever witnessed uproar over issues they agree or disagree with, but what is exceedingly off-putting is no one mobilizes or rallies to correct issues that are happening every single day in the areas of work and love. Those are the areas that the majority of people on the planet tend to be most distressed about over any other Earthly life battle.

I have forever had immense compassion for those in the workforce that are putting in those hours to take care of themselves and their families. I know that it is a means of survival to work hard to stay afloat and keep trudging along. At the same time, many battle and struggle to find that sweet spot center of feeling content while in the whirlwind fight to make it through. This is also a genre and area that my Spirit team has mutually been concerned about. All of this is what pushed this topic to prominence in Earth's history once again. Trends move and shift in cycles throughout the centuries. Human behavior automatically adapts to what is considered the norm at that time, but it doesn't mean that what you're adapting to is favorable to your soul's well-being. Working so hard to ensure your bills are paid can leave your soul spiritually starved for what is more important to your survival, which is soul nourishment.

Talking quick statistics, out of the over seven billion people living around the planet right now, about half of that number are full time employed, with the unemployment rate being in the two to three hundred million ranges. This is a generalized estimate due to how accurate or inaccurate stats can or may not be recorded. There are millions of births each year that do not get recorded. It's impossible to know what every single person on the planet is up to. Some live in circumstances where recording their information with the government is not an option.

Billions of people all over the planet are struggling in jobs they don't care for, or they're trying to find any kind of work, while others hold out for a job they can get somewhat excited about to wake up each day to go to. There are only a handful or small percentage of people around the globe who are working in jobs or careers they love, or one that is their passion and life purpose, while others work in jobs just for the paycheck, which crushes their life force. You also have those without a job trying to find work or some way to make money, which also crushes their life force. When your ultimate goal is to obtain enough money to be comfortable, then there is little to no room for spiritual nourishment and enrichment. The other demographic are those unable to find any kind of work, with some living on the streets or in extreme poverty. No one marches or protests over any of that either.

It is no wonder materialism dominates the planet. This is because money is needed to survive and function without worry or fear. Even those who work full time to make money to survive are merely working day after day all day long for survival reasons. This is to be able to pay their rent or mortgage, put gas in the car, food on the table, clothe themselves, and hopefully have just enough left over to do something fun once in awhile, which might include a nice dinner or a night away somewhere outside of their own home in some other city. This is to break up the monotony, to have some kind of release, and to experience even a sliver of joy and fun.

In the United States, the employment rate peaked in 2000, before it gradually declined until it reached the lowest it had ever been in 2011, then it began to steadily improve, but never reaching the highest employment rate it had reached in the 2000 year to date.

I've been in the business work force for thirty years and grew up in a working class home with two working parents who worked paycheck to paycheck just to buy the basic necessities to stay afloat. There were times they had a hard time doing that. On a spiritual level, I'm also a lifelong clairaudient and claircognizant, with some measures of clairsentience and clairvoyance. This is nothing different than what anyone else can do, since all are born with various spiritual gifts. I've been forever connected with a council of guides from above stating numerous profound foresights of what's happening and what's to come. These revelations have also come true in the end. On top of that, I've been studying the human condition since I was a child. None of this is about rattling off my resume credits for the sake of bravado, but it's more about articulating that I have a grave understanding of the realities, the pitfalls, the struggles, as well as the blessings that others endure. I know what it's like to live in what some might call the trenches. I understand it exceptionally well from both the practical as well as the spiritual perspectives.

We're going to discuss some rough and tough direct realities, before eventually and gradually lightening up into the middle and endings of this with abundance tips, guidance, and messages. All of this is with the intention of inspiring you to have a newfound outlook about the work life set up today. Perhaps it will encourage or motivate you to implement some positive changes to all aspects of your life where possible.

Living for the weekend is something many in the workforce can relate to regardless of what your personal spiritual related beliefs are. If you have no spiritual connection, principles, or views, there may still be some information in this that you can apply to your daily life, even if it's one sentence throughout this whole thing that contributes something life changing in you. There will be information you already know, stuff that's new to you, content that resonates with you, and some that doesn't.

One's work life is what makes up so many people's lives. I understand how challenging that can be to get through it if you're not happy with the work you're doing, but even if you are happy with it, that doesn't mean you want to spend every waking minute doing it. If you're not a full time worker, or you're unemployed, or you work from home, there is still information that may be of benefit to you, because this is also about incorporating more balance, so that you don't feel so drained all of the time. It can be challenging to balance the professional and personal parts of your life. Even more challenging is having a spiritually based nature, yet you find that you work in situations or for companies that lack in that department.

CHAPTER TWO

The Imbalance Between Work, Personal, and Spiritual Life

Before human made concrete structures, people would physically work outdoors in the fresh air. If they were fortunate enough to reside in a location that had decent sunlight, then that was an added bonus. Exercise, fresh air, and sunshine are essential components to incorporate towards your overall health and well-being. Those conditions in both the past and present will always contribute to longevity, more energy, a raised vibration, and stronger health. Whereas the strict corporate structures with the offices, cubes, or open floor plans under poor lighting and artificial cooling or heating systems instead drain one's life force more rapidly than if you weren't in that environment.

Living for the Weekend

It isn't healthy sitting amongst a crowd of people for a long period of time, because you're absorbing all of their energies. When you work in close quarters with a number of colleagues sitting on top of you day after day, then that can drain some of your energy and life force. What sucks that dry is if one or more colleagues are personalities that you just can't seem to mesh well with. Some people go into an office environment, since it's not like you can just quit and live off a trust fund that doesn't exist. You do the best you can do by being disciplined and strict about what you will or will not accept.

There are companies that house CEO's, executives, management, and decision makers who are in tune enough to push the company to make positive work adjustments and changes to ensure their employees are taken care of. It's still in the lower percentages or complaints wouldn't continue to be on the rise.

When you make sure your employees are taken care of, then your business is taken care of. Who wouldn't want to work in environments that are enjoyable with pleasant people? Not everybody does or every single person on the planet would work hard to ensure that this would be the case. They would do their best to contribute to boosting employee morale. This has been an epidemic for so long that a comedy film classic was made back in 1980 called, *9 to 5*, with Lily Tomlin, Dolly Parton, and Jane Fonda.

The three characters had it with the poor working conditions, hours, and treatment that they took matters into their own hands. By the end of the film, they had created a pleasant working environment that was warmer, friendlier, and more flexible. As a result, for the first time all of the employees appeared happy and even more hard working than they were before due to the morale lifting. We know in reality this is not always the case since so many work environments are considered toxic.

One of the screenwriters of that film later commented that people today would kill for a 9 to 5 schedule. This is because as you are likely aware those hours have been increased to 8-5, 9-6, or 10-7, and in other cases it's more than that. You can forget about improving your well-being, or having a life if you're working a tough schedule five days a week until you pass on from this plane. Compounding to that unstoppable work schedule is if you work in toxic environments. That's an added disadvantage that most people could do without.

The positives of the technological age post 2000's is that it shifted how efficiently one works by giving wider options and flexibility. This mindset is gradually being adopted depending on the company and who is running the show. One of the main problems today is that employers, companies, the government, and people in charge have failed to get with the program by adjusting to the new flexibility that can be incorporated into an employee's life. The United States specifically should be ahead of the curve, but has failed in that arena as well. I doubt there is an employee in the work force that would or could disagree. I certainly never spoke to anyone who disagreed amongst the many I conversed with and interviewed over the years.

Having been out in the field and living that life for decades experiencing and gaining knowledge of what it's like has pushed me to the forefront at being a master at understanding what people go through. This is much like a method actor who dives in and becomes the character by living that life. This is coupled with my ability to connect with Spirit in planes beyond, regardless if you're a believer or not. I've ridden up elevators in sky rise buildings with other professionals who are miserable, tired, growling and grumbling lowly, "Is it the weekend yet?"

No, it's only Tuesday.

It takes centuries for human beings in general to evolve their soul, yet there is still a long way to go. If people are continuing to spend their days fighting, arguing, and bickering over a differing opinion and it's resorted to name calling, then no evolving has taken place. Major lifestyle circumstances pertaining to practical human living also takes centuries of evolution before the smallest measurement of change is witnessed. Look how long it's taken for Earthly conditions and basic human needs to change and improve, such as giving women the right to vote, to legalizing interracial marriage or same sex marriage. To have to rely on the government or other people to grant you legal permission to marry the one you love is unheard of by Spirit. Love is the #1 reason all are here in the end. It's not to work a job you hate until you die.

Pour through history to see how long it's taken for basic human needs to progress. In some countries, they still don't have those luxuries. Many are still being pushed down and denied basic human rights and desires by other people. One of the larger anxieties is the work and career arenas. It's concerning on a grander scale because the human work life takes up so much of one's lifetime in general. It's considered an advantage to get to do the work that is your passion and get paid for it, but most struggle to achieve that luxury because of other people. You can put in the work to help you achieve what you desire, but to an extent it still requires other people's assistance, such as hiring someone to do a particular job, or to get others to purchase your products. Whether you are an introvert or extrovert, you need other people to a measurable degree.

Many talented and gifted individuals around the planet never get that lucky break where they can crossover and transition to doing work they love full time and be financially compensated for it. I've sadly watched many of them either give up and throw in the towel or put it to rest.

They can no longer devote any additional time, energy, and finances towards it. They chalk it up to being a lost cause. They grow frustrated and despondent soon experiencing burn out from all that trying with little to no return for their yearly efforts. They watch others rise to the top of the ranks who are less experienced and who put in less time than they have. This was also illustrated in the 9 to 5 film, where the Lily Tomlin character had been working harder and longer at the company than the man they promoted to a higher rank, played by Dabney Coleman.

If your work were your passion and purpose, then you would do it for free, because you receive immense enjoyment and fulfillment out of it. Any compensation from it is simply icing on the cake.

The former outdated ways of working considered it cool to work around the clock until your life run was complete. The more hours you put in and stayed at the office, the more your ego convinced you that you're doing well, while others measure their success by how much money they have accumulated. This is one of the ego's deceptive tricks.

In the end, you grow older, attract in all sorts of health related issues, or find that you're lonely, ignored, and dejected with nothing much to show for it, except maybe a fat bank account. Upon your human passing, you don't get to take your awards, rewards, or money with you anyway. You don't even get to take your toothbrush. It's also rarely likely you will be remembered or thought of much by the masses. You might be mentioned in history books if you were a popular entertainer that shattered records like Elvis Presley or Michael Jackson, or if you contributed something massive to the progression of human life like Benjamin Franklin or Albert Einstein. But let's face it, how many people are sitting around thinking about any of them?

Living for the Weekend

This isn't to say that there is anything wrong with achieving and striving for success, but there does come a point where one is taking it too far and for no real purpose. Most people are working to survive in jobs they hate because it's the way it is. As a result, they experience and endure all sorts of emotional pain whether it is through depression, sadness, anger, or any other kind of negative stressor. Some silently suffer through this emotional strain gradually killing off their life force. If you don't have a healthy social life and positive fun filled activities and hobbies to balance that burden outside of that, then that can add to the tension. What's it all for if you can't live the life you've always wanted to live? Instead, you spend your days growing forever miserable and broken.

Many people have dreams of achieving basic human needs such as a loyal love partner, a family, a home, feeling joy and peace around the clock, while being financially secure. There are some who have no interest in obtaining a love companion for life, so what else are you here for? To work a job where you spend most of your hours among people you don't really care all that much about? When the job run is over, it's probably unlikely you will think about or remember much about them, nor will they with you. The world spins around and life continues on with or without you.

In some cases, sure you'll remain in touch with a select number you hit it off with on a deeper more profound level, but that's on the rare side. Circumstances do in fact change and people move on for various reasons. Nothing stays the same, goals change, structures are revised, and life continues to move forward. In the end, everyone is on their own personal journey where sometimes we intersect for a spell, while other times we get on the same bus for a much longer period only to hop off to transition down another road at some point.

Discussing the current state of affairs where ones work life is concerned is not about adopting a slacker mentality. It's about working smart and integrating successful time management strategies. Working smarter means working harder in a shorter amount of time, than mediocre working where you're available around the clock. Endless data and studies are available that bring to light the truth that people are exhausted in general.

In the past, I had watched that one employee who seems to be one of the first who arrives at the office, and one of the last to leave, yet they move about looking as if they're permanently exhausted and unhappy. Between overworking themselves and displaying resentment over everyone else who seems to come and go as they please adds to the emotional suffering. Worry about yourself rather than what others are or are not doing.

Nowadays someone who is at the office from morning until night is seen as having no life. Because when you have a healthy happy personal life, you look forward to wrapping up work sooner so that you can enjoy that. Having a healthy positive happy life outside of work helps in making that job you despise somewhat more tolerable than if you didn't have positive activities to dive into while not at work. Even if you love your job, you still need to incorporate that personal fun time outside of that. It will add fun, lightness, great ideas, and rewards to the job as well as yourself.

You might also be that person who loves their job, but is still feeling gloomy or somber and you can't figure out why. You could be the one who has nothing else going on in your life, so you stay at work longer than usual because it's become all that you have. The question is, are you truly happy? What healthy choices will or can you make to change that today?

Over the years, I've also listened to the stories of people

moving into their twenties that complain of being tired all of the time. They're pumping themselves up with caffeine and energy drinks to keep going, but are still worn out and run down. They have a more sedentary lifestyle where they're staring at their phones or computers all day. The more disciplined people that manage to keep a strict schedule will squeeze in regular exercise time, but even they are unhappy and tired in the end. If that many people are exhausted throughout there twenties, then where will they be as they move beyond age forty?

My Spirit team has expressed grave concern about where the current work state is around the world. While they applaud hard work, they despise imbalance because they know this prevents the soul from achieving what they desire while burning out of this life early.

There is a large discrepancy of imbalance between the personal and professional, which is solemnly plaguing the planet in a daunting way. To top it off, many crave human interaction if only in the form of one solid, secure, stable, and loyal passionate friend or lover. Even they spend their lives searching for someone who never seems to show up. They need that pleasant and pleasurable escape that ceases to reveal itself and break them from the sad monotony that is their work life. This soul falters and withers while revealing an aura that grows darker, somber, and grimmer than ever.

There are angels from above doing their best to continue to lift those souls up towards Heaven with minimal or short bursts of success. While guides are the more strict council directing souls towards practical experiences for survival purposes that will enhance and help that soul grow and evolve. They know it can help the soul a great deal if that soul is working in a job position that brings them joy. The truth is that isn't realistic for the millions of people working away around the planet, so you do the best you can to get through it.

The change to the current work life starts from the top. This is because the bosses and superiors running the businesses set the rules and general work environment. When you have a work-a-holic superior, then you can be sure you will be worked into the ground.

In some countries, you're trained early on to thrive for financial success in a career or job. This is especially the case in the United States where you're negatively influenced to believing that the more hours you put in, then the more applause and accolades you will receive from others. Unless you're getting paid extra for the effort you put in, it can eventually feel as if you are wasting your time. Putting more hours in than someone else is not something golden to thrive for as if it's a competition. Continuing with that mindset and schedule will guarantee you check out of this life early. In the end, no superior cares all that much that you're working around the clock. According to others, rarely is much praise or added compensation given over doing that.

A superior might say, "James is always in the office from morning until night and I like that."

Yet, James sees no extra income out of it to justify that empty praise, because praise can only go so far. If you think I'm great, then pay me. Actions speak louder than words in this case.

This same concept applies to relationships. A romantic partner communicates what they want with you, but then down the line it turns out those were empty promises. This is because they did not show you this is what they wanted through action. They darted pointless words that ultimately deceived you in the end.

Monetary success isn't long lasting, but spiritual success is. There's nothing corrupt about being adequately paid for your hard work, otherwise you're being taken advantage of.

Living for the Weekend

This is a physical world that requires money to survive on this planet. It's misguided to believe that money isn't everything. It is true that money is not everything compared to love and good loyal friends that understand you and have your back, but the reality is that money is required to survive on the planet.

It is not immoral to desire to live comfortably where you have your home, a roof over your head, a career or job that fulfills you, your bills get paid without worry, a love partner, or a healthy social circle. When you're taken care of with your physical needs, then it is easier to focus on what others need. When you feel safe and secure, then your vibration is raised within that comfort. This makes you a joy to be around.

The current work climate is to work from morning until night and around the clock until you drop dead. Out of the hundreds I've interviewed, no one likes this, but everybody does it just 'because'. It's what they're trained to do by current society, so they feel there is no choice. This plays a part in the kind of life you're living.

Getting up every morning to sit in rush hour traffic day after day until you die is taxing on your emotional and mental state while tampering with your life force. Your life force is connected to your well-being state. When your well-being falters, then that crushes your life force. The rough wear and tear on ones well-being is the end result.

Your well-being state is important for numerous reasons. When you're happy and healthy, then the more love and abundance you attract in. This also raises your vibration, which broadens your connection with Spirit. That connection helps you receive divinely guided information and inspiration designed to keep you on the right path towards enlightenment. Enlightenment is that contentment space your soul seeks. It is the place you resided in when you were born, but Earthly life circumstances soon dulled that beautiful edge that existed within you. If you have the hope of brightening it up again, then I know how you feel, as I've been in that place in the past myself. I did whatever I could to get that feeling unnaturally, which entailed getting my hands on any toxic addiction possible. I wound up running around in circles chasing a mirage. Only when I tuned back in to my Spirit team was I able to manage life more efficiently.

In the past, when I have been on cloud nine, that was when I saw positive circumstances filter in. When I was down or negative, then either more of that came into my life, or nothing changed at all. To an extent, positive thoughts and mindset do work, but this needs to be backed up with faith and action. It's certainly better than being bitter, angry, and negative around the clock. Which person would you like to hang out with? I'm going to go with the happy loving camper who just wants to have a good time and wants you to have one too.

You need to work to survive, pay your bills, put food on the table, and be comfortably clothed. This doesn't mean you should be working at a job you hate until you pass on from this life. It's understood that sometimes you're at a point where you don't have a choice. It doesn't mean the current work structure needs to be set up in a way that brings down morale and slows down productivity. Even superiors don't want to see that!

When you're expected to regularly work late, or constantly take your work home with you into the night, then this will bring down morale, slow down productivity, and gradually weaken your life force to where you check out of this Earthly plane early. If you're not checking out due to human death, then your well-being is permanently suffering indefinitely until you do check out. This is no way to live and you're certainly not living an Earthly life to be in that state until the end. You're not here to work a job you don't care about. With the billions of people on the planet fighting for the same job, your pickings can be slim as to what kind of work you can do. The other reality is that people around the world work at jobs they despise to pay the bills. It's a means of survival and you do the best you can to get through it. Only a small percentage will break away from that by finding meaningful work they're passionate about. You can be part of that small percentage that does indeed break away as I eventually did. When you feel you hate your job beyond measure, then examine some of the other jobs people do out there that would make you even more dismal. This can give you some perspective by helping you to have some measure of gratitude that it's not as bad as it could be.

Follow your life purpose and seek to do work that brings you joy. There will be ups and downs at any job, just like any relationship, but you can aim to get as close to enjoying yourself with your work as possible.

CHAPTER THREE

Bullying, Rudeness, Assault and Tantrums In the Work Place

There is a line to be drawn between doing meaningful work and getting paid for it, as opposed to pure greed chasing. Where you get into greed territory is when you already have the basic human necessities to survive and live comfortably, yet you continue to fight to obtain more. You work around the clock because you have an unstoppable need to collect as much money as you can. You are driven by the dollar gain even though you are set for life. You work your staff to death, and you're abusive and intolerant. When any of that happens, then a reality check and soul evaluation is needed. If you don't choose to seek that out on your own, then one will be forced upon you at some point in your life. The latter is more apt to happen since something catastrophic would have to take place that creates that wake up call. This is in the same way an addict addicted to drugs or alcohol hits that rock bottom moment where the wake up call is successfully forced upon the person.

One example of where a reality check and forced soul evaluation is thrust upon you surrounds the rise and fall of former Hollywood Film Producer Harvey Weinstein of Miramax and the Weinstein Company. Behind closed doors, he was known by former assistants to be a tyrant on occasion. Working for him you were expected to be on call and available 24/7. This means you have to keep your cell phone on even while you're asleep in the middle of the night. Be prepared to answer it should it ring at an ungodly hour for something ridiculous, otherwise expect to be chewed out, yelled at, abusively reprimanded, or fired if none of that is enough to push you to walk. You can never take the subway or drive through a no cell phone service dead zone. Carry your passport with you at work everyday in case it's suddenly demanded that you accompany him overseas.

Scott Rudin, another Film Producer who has not met the same end result as Weinstein, but has been known by some to be a bully at times as well too. Naturally, popular film actors that have worked with him will dish out glowing testimonials about him, but they gave the same glowing reviews to Harvey Weinstein, until his behind the door abusive ways hit the media in a big bad way. There have been accounts of Rudin being physically abusive, such as throwing objects at you while in a fit of rage. You can forget about caressing your well-being while working for a Weinstein or Rudin type personality. They've got away with abuse antics for so long because of the powerful positions they have in the Entertainment industry. People within the industry and outside of it tend to treat Hollywood talent like royalty. Using these two figures as examples doesn't mean it is resorted to just them. Many superiors in different settings around the world are just as abusive if not more.

It is highly unlikely Harvey Weinstein will produce films in the entertainment industry again due to the numerous sexual assault reporting's and stories made against him publicly by so many of his victims in 2017. It kicked off an array of assault accusations against others in the industry as a result, while forcing Weinstein to resign from his company. The company was hugely successful, popular, and respected for years up until the accusations. Months after the numerous claims, the company ended up filing for bankruptcy.

This is an excellent example of how bad behavior towards other people will eventually catch up with you. If not immediately, then years down the line where your downfall is witnessed due to the karmic thread line that tends to happen if you're not careful about your choices. This affected more than this one man, but everyone around him, including the company, staff, and those who might have done business with him.

These examples include those that work around the clock and know nothing about incorporating balance. Many bosses that are abusive are not just abusive in the verbal, psychological, and physical sense, but they're also abusive about your time and how much work you're expected to put in, which is akin to an underground sweatshop. They have a terrible turn out of staff and assistants sifting in and out of those businesses. When they pass on, will the world remember their legacy? Those that know and have worked with any of them will be aware of some of the films they made, but most of the world has no clue who they are or will even care in the end. The extent that the Weinstein and Miramax name will be remembered is that it was the catalyst that set off the trend of people standing up to bullies in the workplace and winning. Although, work harassment laws had already been in place throughout all of the years prior, but what good are the laws if people were still ignoring them? Many in the entertainment industry have had an endless array of sexual allegations made against them from actors, actresses, to former assistants. One of the positives of the technological age is that bad behavior can no longer be hidden. The negative to that is it also invites in false accusations from meddler's desiring to stir up drama and attention. Being in tune can help one decipher what is true and what is exaggerated, false, or an attempt to discredit someone out of envy, jealousy, or any other negative emotion.

One former assistant to Harvey Weinstein said, *"This isn't just about Hollywood. The reason this has captured everybody's imagination is because it involves glamorous famous people, and because if you were trying to paint a fantasy monster, then Harvey fits the bill perfectly. So it's a perfect media storm, but this isn't about Hollywood. This is about the abuse of power."*

Sexual assault in the workplace is one form of abuse that was brought to light to the public, but the abuse that is severely ignored and happens more often is the other kind of ill-treatment: Bullying, antagonism, rudeness, emotional and mental abuse. The latter is done as if it is acceptable by society to behave that way. It's amazing how prevalent unwanted harassment and sexual behavior is in the film industry, but that's just the tip of the extremities. Highly targeted is abusive behavior in general by many superiors and some co-workers in all industries. This includes disrespect, aggression, bullying, and callousness towards staff members. Employees put up with it and take the abuse out of fear of telling anyone or jeopardizing their paycheck to physically survive.

There are bosses from Hell in every industry small and large leaving employees in permanent anguish and turmoil. This is a scary fear to have not knowing what to do or who to turn to. It's amazing that after years of abuse in many companies that no one has come forward to bring that to light in a bigger way. No one mentions the endless abuse and bullying in general by superiors or specific toxic colleagues. Many stay quiet out of fear they will never work again, or because they don't know what else they're supposed to do. It's been made to be acceptable and part of the norm. The bullied employee fears losing that paycheck and not being able to pay their bills, so they dejectedly continue with the job position. That is until they're fired or they snap and are abruptly forced to quit. Some don't report it as they feel nothing will be done, or that it will backfire and the harassment will increase.

I've also listened to and witnessed others who are allegedly writing about anti-bullying in the media, yet they're personally known to be abusive and rude in general. That's a scary thought that someone in the media has that kind of power to manipulate readers by talking against something that they do themselves.

At some point the breakdown of the employee's mental health begins to deteriorate due to the stress and unhappiness that results out of it. The older you get, then the harder it will be. Men tend to have a harder time with it than Women, and part of that has to do with the fact that Men seem to be less vocal about how they are feeling. This is a generalization and a stereotype, because of course it's not true for every single member of that gender, but more often than not it tends to be the case.

Abuse and toxic environments run rampant in the workplace of so many companies. Most employees are afraid to say anything for fear of rocking the boat, confrontation, retaliation, not being believed, or making the work situation worse than it already is. One person might find them to be overly sensitive, while a less than sensitive person will roll their eyes, "Why do they have to start drama?"

As a result, the employee remains quiet with the fear and worry festering underneath indefinitely until they snap or quit.

Bullying and abuse exists in every work industry, but offensive behavior exists around the world in general outside of the work life as well too. It occurs within the confinement dynamics of families, friendships, and relationships. It is also present all over social media and media sites, or when you venture out in public, or bump into people wherever you are. It's no wonder many sensitive in tune people have been vocally stating they want to write others off in general, because who wants to live in that toxicity?

There are people that rather enjoy residing in the darkness of ego. You can pop onto any social media platform and read the posts or tweets that people put up. It's typically bathed in negative dark toxins full of people complaining, ranting, or attacking others one after the other. Rising above the nonsense to look down on the overall behavior of humanity is a bleak and scary view. It's always been this way, but now it's just blown up due to the rapid way information is able to be put up by anyone and their grandmother. No one pays much attention to the good or the compassionate. They want the dirty, the dark, and the mean.

TREATING OTHERS WITH RESPECT

I've worked alongside and dealt with numerous high-powered talent and studio executives in the entertainment industry throughout my twenties before becoming an author. In general, the people I worked with or chose to directly work with were pleasant, loving, friendly people that were a joy to work with. This included both the behind the scenes players as well as the known talent. Those I chose to work with also did not work around the clock. They still managed to get the job done just as well as the tyrannical toxic bosses in the industry. This only proves that you don't need to be abusive or tyrannical to get something done. In fact, it was the pleasant superiors where I noticed more was getting done, because people wanted to put in more work for that pleasant person. When someone likes you, they want to do more for you.

If you're looking for another job or dreaming of getting out of the current job you're in, then try and find a job you love working at for a boss who has a life outside of work. If a boss does not have a life outside of work, then they will be working double the time to make up for that. More often than not, they will expect you to live at your job as well too.

This is by all means not about adopting a slacker mentality. Many of my former bosses and superiors have described me as being one of the most calm and hardworking people they had ever come across. I did that by adopting the strict methods I discuss. I expect respect without asking for it, and I won't work around the clock, but while I'm with that company and during the time agreed, I give my 110%.

The reason I never personally experienced any abuse with anyone I worked with in the entertainment industry could be perhaps I was lucky, chose well in who I'd work with, or because I would never tolerate it. My stance is that I've always demanded mutual respect no matter who the person is or what role they are. I don't care if you're the Pope or the President. You better be respectful and I will give you that same compassionate respect in return. It's the overall demeanor conveyed when I enter any space. This means other people sense it and automatically take notice and oblige in the same manner, including the ones that others have called difficult. I was this way with the star of the film, to the production assistants, to the grips, to the drivers, to the craft service crew, and on and on. No one ever noticed my personality shift no matter who I was working with or talking to. I treated everyone with equal respect. Not everyone follows that mantra. Adopt the method of treating everyone equally and with respect.

Part of the reason I managed to be lucky enough to work with people in the business that were not bullies was that I always took the job interview process seriously. I never looked at the interview as being just about them interviewing me, and hoping I would get the job. I was interviewing them too, and in many cases more so than they were with me. I made it known about the schedule I would not work, which is no around the clock stuff. While I would not expect my potential boss to be my best friend, I would tell them during the interview process that I expect a friendly camaraderie where I could feel comfortable and safe enough to speak openly and candidly with them on matters without fear of backlash, as well as they should be able to do the same with me. I would inform them before being hired, *"The only way this can work is if we're together on the same level as a team."*

They all loved that along with the list of mandatory requirements I expected. They ended up hiring me and we ended up having a successful run together, many of whom I remained friends with long after the gig was over with. I didn't just show up with demands, but I backed that up with how hard I would work for them.

One producer I worked with commented that her young daughter couldn't figure out if I was the boss or if her mother was. The lines were so blurred and I appeared to behave and communicate on the same level as the boss that the daughter couldn't tell. Usually in the boss and employee dynamic, it's obvious who is the superior, but that's rarely been the case with me. I'm going to use quite a bit of film references in this. It reminds me of the film, *Steve Jobs*, and how the Kate Winslet character handled her boss Steve Jobs played by Michael Fassbender. She was the only one who behaved on the same level if not more so. It was as if she had some authority and assertive finesse over him, when others were fearful and cowered in his presence. I've trained past assistants to rise up and be on the same level as their boss if they want to last.

The entertainment industry is filled with compassionate loving amazing loyal people, but it's also got egomaniacs and diva-like behavior from all those across the board. Some in the business would have this attitude of thinking that they're God's gift to the universe because they work in films or music. There is a sense of automatic entitlement. There are no rules as to what is appropriate or inappropriate behavior. There was never any kind of Human Resources handbook guide that would contain harassment protective clauses while filming a movie in those days. There was no Human Resource Director existing on a film production shoot to keep people in line, including the Above the Line crew (actors, directors, producers).

If an Above the Line crewmember such as an actor, director, or producer was a tyrant or abusive, the entire crew would suffer and just put up with it. Whereas in some companies today in some states or countries, new harassment laws have finally been put in place to force people to behave, since people do not know how to behave with respect on their own without being told. With that said, I was never personally victimized by anyone on a film set or in the industry. For the most part I would say 99% of what I witnessed was consummate professionals at work. They were never disrespectful towards me, but I had heard stories through the grapevine about incidents that happened on other film sets, with talent, executives, or production companies that made me cringe.

The Director, Producers, and Stars set the tone of the film production and it gets trickled down from there. This is the same way that any company runs. It is with the top boss setting the tone for the whole company. If the top boss is a maniac, then you will have a super uncomfortable work environment. If you're working with non-professionals or diva like behavior from any of them, then that will create a ripple effect. If the top people are a pleasure to work with and convey a sense of beautiful professional polite calm, then that uplifting energy will also trickle down to the staff making it a pleasurable experience for all. Everyone will notice and feel the vibe in the room as being a wonderful place to work. This was the tone I set whenever working in many of those past companies.

There is bullying behavior by superiors in all industries, but also from people in general. Just go to any comment section online or read a media piece. Most people are not nice and are into gossiping, attacking strangers, or being antagonistic. It is no wonder I've heard so many beautiful sensitive's around the world state they've had enough of this planet. It's thanks to being born, brought up, and having to survive with toxic people around them who operate primarily from the darkness of ego. People are different on all levels from their interests to their values and lifestyle choices, but that doesn't give one license to be disrespectful.

As with any issue, those that claim to care about assault and abuse cases need to make it their lifelong fight. You don't pretend to care for an issue one day because it's the top trending story, while being led like a herd of cattle to the next top story. If it's something you truly care about, then stay focused on it indefinitely making it your purpose and fight to do what you can to produce positive change. Sticking with one purpose and goal without ever wavering shows that you do care about the issue.

Many sensitive's have reached out to me unable to figure out why it's so difficult and challenging for someone to be cordial, classy, and respectful with others no matter what. Earth is filled with egomaniacal, tantrum ridden, drama causing children of all ages in power. They desire constant excess and that mentality will turn dark to the point of greed and power. When one moves into the obsession of greed and power, then they eventually turn into monsters. These are souls that operate through the darkness of ego. Navigating through those endless dark, choppy waters is challenging. As a sensitive, you take in and soak up more than the average person. It can feel like a curse, but you are gifted more than you know. There is a reason you agreed to be here, even if it doesn't feel that way. You can take steps today to be strict about how you govern your life and who you allow into your vicinity whenever you can help it.

CHAPTER FOUR

Driven to Excess and Complaining Into Abundance

The one positive that comes from excess is when it's used to help others. The hoarding of excess creates a block because hoarding comes from fear that you'll lose what you've obtained. An exception is when one is saving up to eventually make a big purchase such as a car or home. The opposite end of that is squandering, which is giving more away than you're receiving. This indicates an imbalanced free wheeling carelessness of waste that ends up coming back to bite you. As with most anything, finding that happy medium balance is the epicenter to aim for. It is where free flowing positive energy and abundance effortlessly streams into your world.

Those successful at achieving excess have learned to distribute and help those of lesser means in some way. This is not done deliberately to create a balanced energy, but rather out of kindness and compassion. They're not lost in the abyss of this excess, but instead have a grounded nature that helps them to see the reality that while they are blessed, others have not been so lucky. They know that they're in a position where they can help those less fortunate than they have been.

Adopt the rule of quality over quantity in all your dealings. In today's world, excess has been glamorized and made to be the only thing that matters. Some people enjoy watching the lifestyles of the rich and famous in entertainment shows. Take away a person's excess to reveal what is left of that person's humanity. This is the true test in witnessing someone's authentic spirit. Sometimes there won't be much left there, but other times you may be surprised to find that there is. When one suddenly gets super rich, it can be easy to lose sight of real reality. You naturally expect that things will be taken care of when you ask.

Excess and greed are witnessed on numerous levels and avenues around you in every possible form beyond money accumulation. It can be that person who tries to see how many matches they can get on a dating app, or how many friend requests they can get on their social media page, to how many followers and likes they can get on posts, pictures, and pages. It's become a tedious numbers game giving you the delusion of believing that what indicates success is how many you have rallying around you online. This is deceptive, false, and fleeting success that gives you the temporary illusion that you are successful. It rarely indicates monetary success, because those with less of an online presence and social media following tend to have accumulated more finances than their counterparts.

Much of this has to do with the fact that those with less of a presence tend to be too busy creating and producing behind the scenes to be posting and amassing followers.

This productivity is what is making them more of a financial success than the younger social media wizard with hundreds of thousands of followers. This isn't the same as a big name brand that will have that kind of following due to the infamous corporate known name or celebrity that they are, but this is about the average person on social media. The social media wizard has achieved ten million followers and likes, but is working a regular job that gives them just enough to pay their bills. They have more time to be posting every hour using all of the *Hashtags* they were trained to use, but it's not translating to financial success. It's merely stroking their ego that so many strangers seemingly like them. But do they like them enough to purchase a product they're selling? The product the social media wizard is selling is usually themselves. They are the product acting as the pied piper to their trail of followers or admirers, but that doesn't translate into financial or spiritual success. It's not making the person much money if any, so they're not a financial success, but that may not be their intent. And because it's stroking their ego in believing strangers love them, it's robbing them of authentic spiritual success.

Ultimate authentic success surrounds your soul's growth and evolving process. It's when you realize that none of the physical ego driven desires matter in the end. You can work hard to make sure you stay afloat and are able to pay your bills and support your family, but you're not chasing friends, likes, followers, fans, or people to prop you up. Any amount of goodness displayed from your heart is the true measure of real accomplishment.

COMPLAINING INTO ABUNDANCE

One of the personal questions many have asked me is how did I get the jobs I wanted. How did I get out of work situations that were undesirable? The first thing that always comes to mind for me was prayer. I know some people don't believe in prayer, but when I've prayed or asked for Divine assistance, that was when the assistance eventually came. I wouldn't force-feed you prayer if it never worked for me. I'm also not insisting that anyone pray, except that prayer works for me. And if you're a non-believer, you're praying without realizing it. When your thoughts move into a plea or gratitude, then you've moved into prayer. You might call it an affirmation or just something you were thinking of. It doesn't matter because the Universe and Heaven is hearing you. They will also hear you when you're incessantly complaining. Complaining that nothing is happening for you or changing for you, as if that will suddenly bring in the blessings.

Complaining your way into abundance will not result in success. If you're going to continue complaining about something, then don't bother praying for it since the complaint will negate the prayer anyway. You ask for heavenly help, but nothing comes around as quick as you'd like it if at all, so you assume you've been given up on. You might play the victim card that no one was able to help, and that you're being ignored, and woe is me. You're trained to stand tall, pull yourself up by your bootstraps, and forge on forward fearlessly.

When you find your faith wavering and well-being crumbling, then lean on your Spirit team for assistance, support, and guidance. Work on being grateful for the blessings they've helped you with to date. Do you have clothes, food, and a roof over your head? Then say,

"Thank you."

God or any enlightened being around you is not Santa Claus longing to drop gifts in your lap the second you ask for it. Some people are under the impression that the job of heavenly helpers is to grant your desires like a genie in a bottle. When that doesn't happen you automatically assume they must not exist or you're being ignored. You're expected to do the work yourself. Sitting around on your couch drinking a beer all day watching a sports game hoping gifts will fall from the ceiling onto your sofa is never going to happen. It's also not Heaven's job or anyone else's job to constantly tell you what to do, where to go, and when to do it. It's your job to do those things. You're given what you need, not necessarily what you want. Needs are the essentials such as housing, food, and clothing.

Spirit guides will step in when necessary to nudge you to move in a certain direction where the most benefit for your soul's growth exists. They will not live your life for you. You're not a puppet on a string that they're controlling. They are like any good best friend who taps you on the shoulder to get you to notice something important, but it's not their burden to carry if you fail to detect it. They can put the same repetitive cues in front of you to get you to see something, but there's nothing more they can do if you're not paying attention to it. If you don't make moves and go after what you want, they are not going to do it for you. If you don't have the confidence to go after what you want, then confidence gaining skills is one of your life purposes to master. Avoiding action steps towards making something happen or making decisions on your own is something you must learn to overcome.

Complaining is surrounded with undesirable energy, which lowers your vibration. It grows into a form of disease since negative anything will manifest into health-related concerns down the line. Sometimes you fall into perpetual daily complaining that you don't even realize you are doing that because it's become habitual.

A journalist repeatedly writes about anti-bullying, but is personally known as a toxic complainer. According to the journalist's colleagues, most of what the journalist says in person is a toxic harsh complaint coupled with assaulting judgment. That toxic energy grew and manifested astronomically by marinating into the cells and pores of this person's physical, emotional, and spiritual body. This is followed by the complainer becoming indefinitely one with it.

You likely know someone like that, and therefore you can understand that it's a challenging person to be around. Especially when you have no choice, but to face them in a workplace environment. Having an understanding that the person can no longer help it and has fallen into the harsh realities of working, can offer some measure of light in how you navigate around someone like that. The best thing to do is avoid or ignore them as much as possible, unless absolutely necessary such as when it's work related and you have to ask or answer a question.

This isn't to say there isn't anything to complain about. The most enlightened being is mumbling a complaint to themselves on occasion as well too. The difference is they are aware when it happens, so they quickly work to shift that complaint into a positive action. They are on the opposite end of the complaint spectrum as opposed to the previous media writer scenario description discussed. Evolving souls prefer to hang around people that complain less rather than hang with a toxic complainer. Evolving souls don't have much tolerance for that kind of negativity and will get out of there as quickly as possible.

Day to day issues happen to everyone all around the planet. Some of it can be extreme enough to push you to vent. Even the nicest, sweetest, most compassionate soul complains. This isn't about that, but about being aware and conscious of when you fall into a dark pattern of daily repetitive complaining that it's become all that you are. When you find that you've fallen into perpetual complaining that it's now annoying you, then work on turning that complaint into action steps. An action step can be choosing to stop complaining. It can be to look at what you're complaining about, and finding creative ways to resolve whatever it is you're complaining about. If it's something that is not realistic or able to be resolved at that point, then work on letting it go. Divert your focus towards positive beneficial activities to distract your mind from the negative, while adding what you desire to your prayer request.

WORK SMARTER NOT LONGER

Full time is considered forty hours a week in many areas. This doesn't include a one hour break in between, nor commute times, so factor in an additional 2-3 hours a day on top of that, which rounds out to about 50-55 hours a week. That is how much time you're technically putting into your work life. Where is the balance? It's no wonder millions of workers are all burned out. There is no life force left, it's gone.

Glum unhappy faces sit in their cars in a parking lot that barely moves, riding up elevators together miserable, scrolling on their phones even though it's not turned on. Many are either single or in unhappy relationships. Part of that is due to the sad state of their work life, which creates a rippling side effect preventing a good love relationship from taking flight and evolving.

You're living for the weekend, but nine times out of ten

you're still burned out throughout the weekend to dive into any fun. In the many interviews I conducted, many would say they don't do much, but lie around the house on weekends. Basically resting up so that they can proceed again at the job they despise. Drinking, partying, doing drugs doesn't count, as that's escaping. This isn't said in judgment if anyone partakes in that, since that is what I used to do in my early to mid twenties, so I understand you're doing what you're trying to do to cope. When I would fall into that cycle, I had to ask myself, is there anything positively benefiting me in the end by having these weekly benders, or am I still miserable? I soon realized it was the latter.

If you're receiving work related emails after your shift is over, then you're technically working and still on the clock. A marketing person explained to me that he was getting emails from a client at midnight. The client was still up emailing requests at that outrageous hour. Until the work force in general is with the program, then no progress will be made. It's one thing to choose to work around the clock on your own, but it's entirely out of line when you're dragging other people into your madness. I'm saying this as a work-a-holic Type A personality where productivity is my thing, but in those instances I'm choosing to do that because it's what I love. And I'm also incorporating disciplined breaks for fun and lightheartedness.

When I was working on film production shoots, before getting hired I would ensure that I would not be working more than 12 hours a day. 12 hours a day on a film shoot is not unusual. Any more than that is an outrageously long day. Employers, the studios, executives, producers all agreed to that beforehand knowing this about me. It was never an issue for anyone. They could've chosen not to hire me, but within the business for that position I was considered one of the best, so they granted my limited minor requests. I wouldn't have accepted the position anyway otherwise. There were exceptions on a couple of film shoots where I stayed an hour or two later max, but that was on one rare occasion in a 100 day shoot towards the end before a long holiday break, so that's not bad. There is a difference between having a great work ethic, to being work obsessed because you don't have anything else going on in your life. If you don't have anything else going on in your life, that's not anybody else's problem, and they most certainly shouldn't suffer because that's the life you choose to live.

When someone's work has become their life, then all other parts suffer from family, friends, lovers, relationships, and your health and well-being. That's a major sacrifice that is not worth anything in the end. There is no real time off, and the time off taken is usually spent working at some point that day. Rarely does anyone go away these days because of the lack of time, energy, and/or money.

Many respectable hard working good employees will leave their job if they have had enough. When they receive a jolt of fearlessness to rip the Band-Aid off, then they will take a leap of faith and quit their job. It's become challenging for companies to replace them since the new crop of up and comers grew up during a time where they were told they could be anything they wanted to be. The reality is that only a small percentage will achieve their ultimate dreams and desires, but it doesn't hurt to try and become that small percentage.

People cheer as their favorite pop star shouts like an evangelical preacher on stage that you can be anything you want to be. Basically, you too can sell hit records and purchase a mansion to live in. Except in reality, more people than not will be struggling in jobs or in finding a job as something to do to get by, but one that is not their ultimate passion.

How about people in third world countries? Can they be what they want to be living in conditions that are difficult? The conditions they live in are their only perspective of life. Many of them can still be spiritually healthy with strong communities, friends, and family, while an American may have achieved wealth, but is spiritually bankrupt and without love, family, or community.

Believing you can be anything you want to be is an exceptional perspective to help you thrive and at least give yourself a great shot at achieving what you agreed to this lifetime. It is not a far-fetched notion that you can conquer your dreams as other great successes have. It is better to believe in yourself and what you are capable of than to not do so.

CHAPTER FIVE

Miserable Commutes and Generational Influences in a Work Environment

A super high number of people complain about the daily rush hour traffic they endure to get to and from work, with the bulk of the complaints coming in from those living in big cities. When you take a step back to examine it, then who can blame them. You're sitting in a parking lot that barely moves twice a day five times a week. It takes you longer to get to work or to get home than it should. You miss out on life because by the time you get home your entire physical body and well-being is worn out from the traffic.

There are also now endless studies and statistics indicating that sitting in long commutes packed with traffic on a regular basis has a negative effect on your mental health and well-being. Before those studies, others would brush it off that it is what it is, or to get over it. It can be challenging to get over something that is tampering with your physical, mental, and spiritual health on a daily basis. This is something my Spirit team and myself had illustrated and warned about in my earlier works, but is still an ongoing unresolved issue because it would require a massive change on a global scale from those in power.

Miserable commuting to and from work is sometimes the worst part of someone's job. Try sitting in a parking lot 10 times a week to drive 15 minutes, but that takes you an hour. That's a mental fight braking and accelerating, braking, and accelerating every few seconds. You have people fighting to turn onto a street where there is no room for another car. You're enveloped by that ferocious dark energy from the people and cars all around you closing in on your soul. You start to feel your anxiety and blood pressure rise, which soon goes nuclear prompting bouts of road rage. By the time you get to work you're already exhausted and worn out from the battlefield that is the current road situation. By the time you get home, you're too tired to do anything. You have a bad attitude and that transfers to whomever you live and work with. These lengthy struggling commutes make it challenging for many to enjoy life.

Most people have to commute because the only place they can find a job is in an area they can't afford to live in, thereby creating horrid commute times. This affects every aspect of your life. It affects your job performance, so the company suffers too. Poor performance, poor morale, poor everything all around. The ones in power who can change this set up don't make necessary changes such as more flexible work hours, work set ups, or affordable housing within that area. It's amazing that no one mobilizes to protest that either, but will jump into time wasting protests over superficiality or triviality that changes nothing. The current break your back work state affects millions of people that would love to see a change implemented. There wasn't one person that I interviewed who didn't disagree.

You could leave work happy and excited, but by the time you arrive at home after sitting in a mess that moves one inch every five minutes, you wind up miserable and exhausted. It's understandable you find yourself complaining about it. You probably tell yourself that you can't help it, but what can you do about it? What can you do if you're complaining about it every time you get into the traffic?

Some may want one easy answer, but the reality is there is no easy answer and deep down you know this. Maybe you have to do it all alone. There is no supportive loving companion when you get home so that you can smile, embrace each other in a hug, communicate about fun activities, and lighten the burden on your soul as a result. Sometimes it's the little things like that for some people that make all the difference in the world. It can help when you have other upbeat fun activities outside of work and those drawn-out commutes to partake in.

Many have chosen to do certain tasks while sitting in traffic. This includes listening to podcasts or books on tape, while others listen to music, or catch up on phone calls to pass the time, safely that is with an earpiece. The rebuttal is that doesn't necessarily reduce the stress of sitting in traffic because some personalities are still aware of the congestion while listening to their content of choice. Gradually, your focus moves away from what you're listening to, and onto how late you're going to be sitting in that traffic. It takes exceptional discipline and fortitude to re-train your thoughts when you're about to lose it in that traffic to somehow get yourself as close to that loving centered space as much as possible.

All those distraction techniques temporarily work if it's a riveting diversion that doesn't take your eyes away from the road. Someone might suggest to others to lighten up about the traffic since you can't do anything about it, but it's still a major complaint by many workers out there. The effects and weight of sitting in traffic like that will be vastly different between someone who has been riding in gridlock traffic for two years, to once in awhile, as opposed to someone who has been doing it for twenty-five years, twice a day, and five days a week.

I'm sure this all sounds like one big complaint so far, but this is a major concern for so many people that it needs to be discussed. People nominate and vote in Presidents, rulers, and people in congress in hopes that person will change their life, but little is changed. Certainly what matters and affects millions of people has most definitely never been changed. This includes the work lives of millions of people coupled with affordable housing rentals.

You could find a job closer to home or move closer to work. If that we're doable you would've done that by now. It's often far more expensive to live near one's place of work. There is a grave disconnect between work pay and the price of places to live in that vicinity. This is why so many wind up stuck in miserable commutes. While others move to new big cities not knowing about the reality of how bad the commute will be. On a map, it can look as if the place they found to live is super close to work. That is until they move and discover the horrific reality of their new set up.

It's not an unfathomable idea to work hard to change your situation, but it will be a fight and struggle for some, while others never see much movement. Let's say you leave your job to accept another one that is closer to home.

The worst-case scenario is you give up a job that you loved or one that was at least acceptable in order to be closer to home and avoid the Hell commutes, but then the new job is one you end up despising.

When movement doesn't come to pass after numerous years, then this can shake your faith and push you to become permanently glum about your situation. You start to doubt the existence of all things otherworldly such as God, your Spirit team, Heaven, and the Universe in general. It's a natural ego reaction to begin placing blame, "Well, if they existed they would help me."

Is it their job to do that? How would you help you if you were in their shoes? And help you with what exactly? Get you out of a situation you chose to be in at the hands of your own free will? The other side of that is you are in that situation for a reason that will benefit you if not at that moment, but later on down the line.

In my own past work life, every job I accepted since I was a teenager had given me additional skills I did not have when I started the job. This led to the other things I've accomplished throughout my life. It was only long after the job was complete that I looked back in hindsight and realized why I was at that job at that particular time.

You're developing or perfecting certain skills you might not think much about. Someone can be a relatively shy person, but after they work a good run at a retail job they find they're less shy and more confident than they were before the job. It can be subtle changes that you don't notice until you look back on it.

Your Spirit team will keep you safe when you ask for guidance. They will guide and assist where it's possible within their means of being able to do so, but it is up to you to stand tall no matter how tough life can be. Lean on them for support, stay strong in faith, ask for repetitive daily help, pay attention to the signs in your path that require you to act towards this positive change, then take those action steps to get the energy moving.

GENERATIONAL INFLUENCES ON WORK LIFE MODIFICATIONS

The average person tends to hate or despise their job around age thirty-five and above more than any other age. There are various reasons for this, which includes things like if you're not where you thought you would be by that age in your career, or you're not engaged in meaningful work. If it's become just a paycheck to survive, then you will grow miserable, unless of course you have a natural sunny disposition. I've come across naturally sunny disposition people and even they may be putting on that face to the world, but inside they are feeling down about things. They're just putting on the pretend false face.

For others, it's working in environments that are hostile or toxic, which leads to a rise in hatred for their job, boss, colleagues, or all of the above. You might love the job itself, but not one or more of the people you work with. Those are traits that as you age the average person tends to have less tolerance for. Finding meaningful work is like looking for Mister or Mrs. Right.

Being gossipy and cliquey seems to sadly be the norm when you're a teenager or in your early twenties, but as you age you hopefully evolve out of that with some measure of maturity. Unfortunately, that is not always the case. This also means that you're turned off by gossip and negativity in any form. If you're not, then that's something you'll want to do a thorough evaluation with. Those working happily with their life purpose or in jobs they love tend to be less attracted to that, and more attracted to focusing positively on their work. If you're unhappy with your work, then you're more likely to be attracted to or drawn to gossip or negativity without realizing it.

A great many workers over the age of forty are being laid off or fired. This isn't necessarily due to lack of poor performance, since that age group tends to be more experienced than any other, but they do make more money than the younger generations. Companies will let those older with higher wages go in order to save money if they're hurting. They'll just have the younger up and comers do it for less money. Take a look at the people where you work and notice how many people are over forty. For many companies, it is likely that there are not as many as there once were.

People born around the mid-to-late 1990's and into the early 2000's are what some people call, *Millennials*. These are people that were the first to be born and brought up during the rise of the technological age that included the Internet, smart phones, computers, etc. While those things were gradually popping up in the years and decade before that, it didn't really blow up until the Millennials were born. As a result, the mentality is significantly different than the previous generations.

A greater number of people have been taking on the flexible temporary work schedule. There are various names used for this such as, "Gig Economy" or "Alternative Work". Some of what this entails consists of working as an independent contractor or freelancer where you are hired to take on one temporary gig after another on your own schedule by an outside firm. The positive side to this is for those who desire a flexible working schedule, which a growing number do. The con or challenge is that it's not steady long-term employment for those seeking full time job security. This could potentially create an unstable work setup for some folks, while being ideal for those that fear being tied down to a particular job for the rest of their life.

I came from the generation era where it was common to be employed by a company for years, and for some even decades. If it looked like you had been with a company for a long period of time, then this looked good for you in the eyes of companies seeking to hire permanent staff.

This has been reversed since a growing number of the Millenial generation specifically has seen shorter job term stays on their resume. They're not staying with companies for a lengthy period of time as the generations passed did. Having spoken to Human Resource Directors at various companies, they all informed me that they do look at how long someone has been with a company, and that does play a factor in their hiring process. Regardless that the trend has shown younger people staying at their jobs less, it's still frowned upon in the eyes of employers at major companies looking for folks who will stay for awhile, if not indefinitely.

The largest job opportunities increased in the areas of the alternative work set up around 2005-2015 specifically. This indicated an enormous growing trend that the work life set up was slowly changing in some areas due to the positives of the technological age.

The world's population continues to multiply rapidly more than in centuries past. If this continues like a runaway mine train, then this will create a catastrophic problem. There are more births than there are deaths. People are taking better care of themselves, and as a result end up living longer. The death rate isn't matching the accelerated birth rate. One of the numerous issues this creates is more competition with less available to help people survive. Some people will be cut out of the work pool. If they're not saving money early on, then this will create another problem as they move into older age. When there is no more money coming in over a certain age and you're living longer, where will the funds come in from to continue surviving? These are things that no one thinks much about until it's too late.

The population on the planet is beyond capacity and with that comes a lack of jobs and opportunities. There are more people fighting over the same job. Pay is low and housing and rents continue to climb each year. More people than not are living with a roommate or more, or they're still living at home. This is not a reflection that they're a failure, but is instead about the fact that the world has changed dramatically. It's become near impossible to survive on ones own unless you're a successful doctor, lawyer, investor, or movie producer.

The older you get, the more risky it feels to make a drastic move such as an employment change. As one moves into the 30's and beyond it can grow or feel more difficult.

This is a world where age discrimination reigns, and employers seem to be more apt to hire someone young and inexperienced for cheap, over someone older with tons of experience, but with more baggage and more money. Factor in if you're older and have been at your company forever, then you fear losing the benefits you've accrued. There are endless factors you have to take into account before making an extreme decision.

Today, older seniors are ignored by society and ignored on the street in passing. Most people don't pay attention to them and no one will hire them. Society used to give respect towards elders, but this shifted when technology grew creating an ageist society. Not only do people not respect their elders, they don't respect anybody, even those deserving of respect. Granted, yes people should earn your respect and it shouldn't automatically be given, but this shunning the older is the overall personality of the masses.

Society overlooks the people that move about through the streets near the brink of ultimate poverty and despair.

These are the older people who have been unable to find work for years. They're ignored on the sidewalk and invisible to the rest of the world. Actress Michelle Pfeiffer played such a character dominating nearly every scene as Kyra in the dark, moody, and realistic film, *Where is Kyra?*

"It's just hard out there. I'm no spring chicken." Kyra says. She is a divorced older woman caring for her ailing mother Ruth. She's been unable to find a job since she was let go from the company she worked at as an accountant a couple of years prior. This is a common theme among so many in the world. Full of definitive rejection, anguish, and despondence she explains, *"Ever since I lost my job, I have been looking for work every day. I don't even know how many resumes I've dropped off. I have tried everything, and am reduced to handing out flyers on parked cars and praying every day that I even have that."*

Kyra's luck grows from bad to worse when her mother passes away. Still unable to find work, she dresses younger and hipper in an attempt to shave years off her age so that someone will hire her. This doesn't work either and she soon ends up on the verge of being evicted from her apartment, leaving the next pit stop to include potentially panhandling and living on the streets.

One uncomfortable saving grace is that her mother's death was never properly recorded, so the government continues to send the social security payments to Kyra's apartment. Kyra dresses up as her mother for bank visits in order to fraudulently cash her mother's disability checks. This isn't about her committing a crime, but what people do when it comes down to basic survival. It's a dilemma that the struggling aging individual hopes they will never be faced with, but one that so many people end up fighting through and enduring alone.

I've always had enormous compassion and interest for those I see fighting to survive and stay afloat. They are the people that are in the background just trying to get their bills paid. *Where is Kyra?* tells the unpopular unheard story of the people that others snub on the street because they may not look like a hot young charming model. They've committed that Earthly crime of aging, while simultaneously dissolving into the background where they are discarded and dead to their surroundings. No one looks at them or talks to them as they evaporate from view.

This art house independent film is an essential social commentary on the sad state that currently exists among so many people. Hundreds of millions of people grow older and struggle to find any kind of work with no luck at all. I've listened to some of their stories, I see them on the streets and sense their pain, while everyone else turns a blind eye disinterested. The older they get, the harder it gets, and this film sheds some beautiful magnificent light on that.

Another film that captured the blending of generations efficiently in the workplace was Nancy Meyer's, *The Intern* with Robert DeNiro and Anne Hathaway. While this one is lighter on the scale, it does show how things could be if older generations were not discarded so effortlessly in life today.

DeNiro plays an older senior in retirement that has money and a successful body of work in his past, but he wants to keep working. He wants something to do and a place to go. He is hired as an Intern at a successful start up company helmed by Anne Hathaway's character. At first, she is reluctant to hiring an older senior seeing the idea as silly. She ignores him in the beginning, but gradually begins to pay attention when she notices positive things he's doing. Soon a beautiful budding friendship develops between them. She finds herself leaning on him for support, and he admires what she's put together in her business on her own at such a young age. The two realize they have positive benefits and assets to gain from one another while in one another's presence. It results in success all around, from success with her company, to the best friendship they have with each other.

Ruling people out because of their age is a grave mistake because generations of people come together with huge age gaps proving that they make an explosive pair when they incorporate their own generational influence into the task at hand.

CHAPTER SIX

Working From Home Remotely and the Work Benefits and Challenges In a Technological World

Millions of people endure long commutes to work at the exact same time five days a week, yet more than half of them don't need to all be heading in at the same time. Many of those jobs can technically be done from home now. The company either doesn't allow it or hasn't thought about it. They may not feel confidant about it due to not trusting the employee to be working while at home. What does that say if an employer doesn't trust their employee? They can still monitor the employees work habits and accountability when they see work is getting done just as efficiently from home as in the office.

Working from home remotely has been an ongoing

trend that started to accelerate around the year 2015. From that point it gradually began to rise. It will soon become the norm whether anyone approves of it or not. Older generations may have a more challenging time shifting in that direction as it's not something they're used to. It wasn't the world they were raised in, but it is the increasingly growing reality that is changing in the work place.

Many have protested that they would love to work from home. This isn't to be mistaken for laziness or being up to no good, because those that work from home still need to be accountable and reachable, or the employee will be let go and replaced. The benefit to working from home or remotely is that you have a break from sitting in regular day-to-day traffic. Statistics have come out indicating that long traffic commutes add stress and disintegrate your well-being and health over time. You walk into work stressed out as a result, which plagues everyone you come into contact with. This also affects your job performance and the company's progression towards success.

Those who do work from home have talked about the positives. They're able to get more done without the constant distractions that would normally bombard you in an office environment. There are fewer interruptions enabling you to focus completely on your job. There is less employee friction with potential toxic colleagues, since you're not seeing or bumping into them to deal with their nonsense.

The downfall to working from home full time is the risk of isolation and working around the clock without incorporating boundaries and balance. Sensitive introverts tend to thrive more successfully while alone. Other drawbacks include the many that work from home tend to get started earlier than usual long before their shift starts. This is primarily because they're already up and don't need to get ready or endure the long stressful commute times if they were going into the office. They also don't know when to quit working, so they end up working longer than their usual schedule without getting paid for it. This is why the work from home remotely option is one of those things that companies have to work with an employee on. The working from home trend has seen an increase in productivity and the employee appears calmer and less stressed out. Part of that is because all of that unnecessary weight and excess fat has been cut out. No lengthy commuting or the mind numbing dreariness of going into an office to stay at around the clock. Incorporating balance is crucial in life.

There are employees that do prefer to go into an office. They don't care to work from home, although those tend to be the older generations who are used to that set up. Human nature is habitual at its core, and change is difficult for most people. This is part of the reason it takes years and sometimes centuries to see the slightest improved progression on Earth. The reality is it will become the newer way of working where more people than not will be working from home in the future.

A company would need to discuss each employees needs along with the companies needs in those arenas. It would entail who prefers to work from home or in the office full time as opposed to part time. Some want to split it up, while others prefer full time at one or the other. The benefits of working from home remotely full time or part of the time will ultimately be an enormous stress lifter for millions of people around the planet. It will also save on high rental costs for companies having to purchase office space and overhead. This is another reason some companies are implementing this work set up for certain jobs if they see that it's more beneficial.

There has been little movement happening in that

direction within the current work culture. Some companies are making the transition of attempting to adjust schedules to make things right. They have been gradually making shifts and changes as far as a more flexible schedule for their employees depending on the nature of the job.

Some old school traditional CEO's prefer to see the persons face and have that personal interaction. Other employers are automatically offering the flexibility of working from home full time or 2-3 days a week while alternating that with coming into the office. This way there is a balance of half and half. They've witnessed a morale boost at the company as well as an increase in productivity because these people are working smarter and harder. The employee is less stressed out as a result. This translates positively towards the growth of both the employee and the company.

The benefit to this set up of working from home is that there will certainly be less traffic on the roads if half the city is at home working away. Employee morale will be up since they're not stuck in one location from morning until night everyday of their life. When an employee's morale is up, they work harder, and the company becomes more successful. When you take care of your employees and treat them right, they will go to the moon and back for you.

Unfortunately, many companies or employers have not evolved into that transition. They are still operating work lives the way they always have. I've worked at companies in the past where more than half the employees had jobs that were done 100% on the computer, yet they were still rushing in to and from the business day in and day out, when their job can be done from home. It started to look a bit ridiculous and absurd. Other companies caught on and offered the flexible work environment schedules for their employees by breaking up their time to half at home and half in the office.

The working class is all in the same boat together. They get up every morning five days a week to drive to a job they don't really care about all that much. You spend all day there everyday for five days straight. Then you have the weekend where you spend most of Saturday trying to get all the stuff done that you had no time to do during the week. You do this angry, stressed, or worn out.

Soon it's Saturday night, which you'll either spend with your family, a lover, pizza and a film, or alone logging onto a dating app trying to connect with someone. This is if you're lucky. Sunday you're depressed because you know it's time to go back to work again on Monday. And this is your life. You go back and forth until something goes wrong with your car or you. Then you have to get some paid time off to take care of it, or you lose your job.

This is the reality that human souls designed. They have not figured out that it's time to change it. Those who have the power to change it are not interested in changing it because they don't live that kind of a life. They are well to do and oblivious to what the rest of the world is stuck in. Any changes they make to the working structure benefit nobody. They don't walk in the employee's shoes and don't know that the change they make will negatively affect that employee, or maybe they don't care. They should care, because if you have an unhappy employee, then productivity and your business will suffer. Who wants to be around permanently discontented employees and colleagues moving about?

There are jobs where you cannot work from home, such as retail jobs, restaurants, or places where you are working with customers in person, or on film sets. This working remotely from home dynamic is about the kinds of jobs where that flexibility and possibility is present.

40-hour work weeks are part of the labor law that was enacted back around 1940. Before that point, people were working 10-hour days. Employees didn't like that schedule and so the work force went on strike, picketed, marched, protested, and tried to get that changed. Congress finally did change that, but look how long that took. This is a positive case where a protest actually worked and changed things. This is because the protest that was happening benefited people from all walks of life regardless of their personal beliefs and values. And now that needs to be changed again.

This dates back to the late 1700's when Americans were working 10 hour plus days. By the early 1800's, they had enough and workers started to go on strike. They were fighting to get it changed to 8-hour days. It was around 1867 when legislature was finally passed to drop it to 8-hour days, but there were still loopholes and issues with that.

By the late 1800's, the fight was gradually operational to allow 8-hour work days. There was a strike that shut down the economy for a week forcing the change to be made. People wanted a drop in hours without a cut in pay, while others accepted the cut in pay in order to work just 8 hours.

The Fair Labor Standards Act was implemented in the late 1930's making the 8-hour work day mandatory as full-time work. Any additional hours worked were considered overtime.

Humankind is at another breaking point as a society. One of the reasons is due to the rise in technology. People are basically on call around the clock and still working beyond normal work hours. Supervisors, Employees, and Clients continue to send work related emails long after they've left the office or after work hours. The second you check your business email on your phone or home computer, you are officially on the clock. It doesn't help that society has drilled into everyone's heads that you should essentially live for the weekend.

A reader named Jack informed me that he receives work related emails throughout all hours of the day. This is on a weeknight, super early in the morning, on weekends, and even on a vacation day off. 9 times out of 10 the email is not urgent even if the sender might think it is. Some people have supervisors that are inexperienced as bosses or managers. They have little previous work life experience and this shows by their actions and the way they communicate. It causes an enormous amount of issues with productivity and morale. At times it can create a toxic atmosphere due to this lack of experience. Everyone in the line of that fire of the inexperienced worker suffers as a result.

Jack is a regular hardworking full time employee in the working class force. We're not talking about a high powered lawyer who might be on a serious case that has him working hard into the wee hours of the night. The lawyer in that case is choosing to work like that for himself in his big house to win the case. He's also getting paid an enormous amount of money for all of that time and energy put into the work. In Jack's scenario, while this isn't to discredit his work position, but it's a position that whatever is being emailed to him off work hours can wait until Monday when he's back on the clock again.

It doesn't matter if you're doing what someone might consider to be menial work as long as you're happy with your job. If you are always stressed out at work, or becoming aggravated, or testy over every little thing, then that is a sign that you don't like your job and are under the delusion that you do. People who enjoy their job have a great attitude about it. They love going in most days.

It's going to continue to get worse until the breaking

point happens and everyone is forced to get on board to make it better. If so many people are now aware of it, then that will snap some sense to change things. At the same time, humanity in general is slow to pick up on positively changing anything. This is evident in past history that indicates how long it takes for people to evolve on issues. It takes them centuries! For that matter, this will be a complaint for years, and perhaps even decades, before trickles of positive change are seen. You just witnessed in the earlier scenario that it took two centuries of the work force fighting to reduce the ten-hour day to an eight-hour day. Although, today it's a nine-hour day and you're still working long after you've left the office with those emails you keep checking, sending, and responding to.

This around the clock work life started growing beyond 2010. This is due to having a technological device, which makes contacting people too easy at any hour. The newer generations were raised on phones doing everything on them. They also transferred this poor etiquette behavior to the work place and everyone followed suit.

Before the year 2010, I would never hear about anything work related until I was physically at work. And in those days I was coordinating film productions for the major studios. Helming a crew of 600-800 people on a $100 million dollar plus film shoots, yet I still had my weeknights and weekends off. Weeknights and weekends were always super quiet work wise. It was strictly devoted to my personal life. Once in a blue moon maybe every six months I might receive that rare work call from a boss, "I'm so sorry to bother you on the weekend, but do you know if..."

Those I let slide because they were rare, and it was a quick two-minute question, as opposed to now for some workers where it is around the clock.

There are many European countries that have it down.

Many of them offering 6 hour work days, which led to the discovery that employees were not only ten times as productive as employees who worked more hours, but they were happier with a radiant infectious well-being state. This filtered that good vibe related energy throughout the company onto others creating a beautiful atmosphere and working environment. They have more energy and are healthier as a result. They have more time to take care of themselves with exercise, better diets, and to connect with friends and family, which also boosts Dopamine levels, morale, and their overall well-being. This also makes them more gung ho about work.

How often have you gone into work where it's a day you have to leave early for something, and you still end up getting what you need to get done? This is because you know you have less time to wrap it up and be out of there. When you know you have a short amount of time to get something done, then you mentally know how to make that happen.

CHAPTER SEVEN

Faced with Toxic People in the Workplace

Balancing career work life and the personal spiritual part of you is no easy feat. Maintaining your personal divine ethics and values when you work alongside anyone who is antagonistic on a regular basis can be challenging. Navigating through the practical based security-seeking world can also present its own set of tests on your soul.

It is not enough to sit back and hope nothing toxic touches you, for it will if you're not careful, but it will even if you're minding your own business. If you're engaging with other people at any point, then you run the risk of bumping into someone toxic. Unless you're a hermit or gypsy living in the woods solo, it's inevitable you'll be communicating with another person as you move along your soul's path.

Governing every part of your life requires a disciplined approach when it comes to the choices you make that can have a positive or negative affect on your auric field and overall well-being. You can control who you choose to communicate with for the most part. The challenges rise when you leave your place and venture off onto the streets to visit areas where another person will come into contact with you. If you live or work in a space with other people, then this will be unavoidable. In those instances you will have no choice, but to connect with them. Even if you keep to yourself or ignore others, you'll still walk past someone at some point and by that action alone you're absorbing their energy. If their energy is toxic or negative, then some of that will contaminate your aura. You cannot work your way around that, but you can be disciplined about how you're engaging with others.

Janelle, a twenty-two year old reader, informed me about her work life at a tech company and how her co-workers are plain awful in general. They would do things like constantly making fun of her for having crystals on her desk. One colleague continually harassed her about it and her beliefs by calling her names like a *Hippie Buddhist.* There isn't necessarily anything offensive about those two words in general, but in this context it is used with derogatory intention. This is regardless that one word doesn't have anything to do with the other. This is an example of what non-spiritual believing people call those who are spiritually based as an attack. I have certainly had that in the past where a string of words created out of a former fad are strung together incoherently. People that don't understand something or someone will usually resort to name-calling.

Janelle has struggled trying to be true and honest about

her beliefs and abilities without jeopardizing her career and having everyone think she's crazy. It shouldn't matter what anyone thinks of you. There will always be someone on the planet that has a problem with you, so you have to get over that. There is no such thing as Universal love, except when it comes to God and Spirit's love for you, since they love you without conditions.

Having bullying behavior in the workplace so late in Earth's evolution is mind-boggling. Notice how bullying behavior continues in every circle and on every platform imaginable today. There are the permanently angry and agitated that create demonstrations over any kind of slight or bullying conduct that reveals itself, yet they are displaying hypocritical intolerance for those with different values and beliefs in their day to day life as it is. They're okay with bullying disrespectful behavior as long as they're the ones exhibiting it.

Accept people for their differences, but have no lenience for disrespect. Centuries into progress and the darkness of ego reigns supreme.

Until every company is forced to become stricter about allowing employees to hold to their personal value system and creative expression, as long as it's not imposing or judging another, then there will always be that rotten apple in the workplace you have to deal with. It's terribly demanding on your soul and well-being working in an environment with just one horrible person, let alone an entire group.

While I have worked with an immense amount of compassionate and talented people, I have also worked with insolent people who are opposing to my personal values and ideals. They're not someone I would engage with unless necessary. Usually avoiding and ignoring them works, but there were rare occasions where someone was antagonizing everyone around them. There was that one repeat offender I had to stomp out and confront. This always quieted them down to the point where they feared me when I'd walk in the room. I have the Wise One attitude, *"Don't make me play bad cop, I don't like it. Do whatever you want when you're not here, but while you are here you will respect and show compassion to every single person you cross paths with."*

It doesn't matter if anyone shares my personal values, but what does matter is if you're disrespectful and unprofessional. Have a zero tolerance policy for disparaging behavior in any form whether it's professional or personal. At the same time working in environments that are exceptionally diverse helps you to adapt to other types of people. This is not telling anyone to accept abusive situations, but working with others who are different from you can be done as long as all parties are professional, courteous, and compassionate.

Working with bad-mannered hostile people creates a toxic environment where everyone in the vicinity suffers. Employee morale drops, life force diminishes, and the company suffers. If prolonged it can permanently destroy all three. Perhaps the company may not care if the morale of their employees drop, or that their life forces are being crushed, but they will start to care if they see their company failing as a result.

What's even more taxing on you is if it's coming from the bosses, executives, and supervisors. They set the tone of the environment that quickly gets trickled downward and spreads throughout the company permeating it with toxicity. They are a superior, which means their superiority over you can intimidate someone that feels they have power over them, but in the end when the job is over with, they have no real genuine power over you. Only you have power over you.

A good boss or executive is aware that their employees

are the backbone of the company from the employee who is at the lowest end of the rank to the highest. All of them matter and are equal in the eyes of a good boss. Everyone is contributing something valuable that keeps the business running smoothly. As a good boss, you want to ensure all employees are considered valuable and crucial to the betterment of the business. You are paying someone for their services, therefore they have value, but all people should have value in your eyes regardless if you're paying them or not.

Navigating the testy waters that can arise in the workplace is often challenging. You being an evolving spiritual person finds that you have to work a job with others who don't share your values. What can make the situation worse is when the people around you are disrespectful to you or to others. If that's not the case, then their energy can contaminate the environment in general. They could be professional with you, yet you consistently hear them stirring up drama elsewhere. Being in someone else's line of fire can wreak havoc even if it's not directed toward you. You're still absorbing that by being in the vicinity.

There have been numerous laws enacted in the workplace to prevent discord. A good Human Resource Director will enforce those laws that you see posted in the workplace break room for a reason. One of the Human Resource Director's instructions may include that employees be careful about the kinds of conversations they have with colleagues while in the workplace.

For instance, you may be talking to your colleague who you know can handle your radical obscenity laced conversation or humor, but someone within earshot may not, and could find fault with it. Lawsuits have been made against companies and employees over things like that in certain jurisdictions where it is considered harassment. This is partly why a great Human Resource Director will work hard to enforce those rules, and not necessarily because they agree or disagree with what happened or what was said. They check those personal values at the door. Their job is to protect both the company and the employee from any kind of legal action or business financial loss as a result of what someone said or did. There is nothing wicked about someone not sharing your values, but what is inappropriate is harassing someone over it or being disrespectful.

Dealing with toxic people in the workplace has been a concern for many employees, including those in the spiritual crowd. This is from those who are into improving themselves and aiming to live a more pain and drama free life. I've listened to stories from those in the spiritual crowd that work in a psychic or spiritually based shop where they also experience toxicity, discord, and drama. I know you would think that a spiritual place of business would be all loving and drama free, but that is not the reality. It is still a business like any other in the end. One particular popular psychic corporate chain store shop has had numerous psychic readers leaving the company to start their own psychic practice. When I asked each of them why they left, their answers were all the same. It was that the company was shady and behaves differently than the intent of the genre. On the other hand it's corporate owned and when that comes to play it's all about business. However, in this case it was about the internal politics.

You could be stuck in an office environment that has an open floor plan, which makes it even more challenging to avoid people you're not interested in engaging with unless necessary. The open office environment only works when you have 3-5 employees. When you have more than that, then it creates chaos making things look more like a furniture store than a business. The reason some companies have made the open office set up a new trend is because people were complaining that the cubicle design seemed to signify a coffin for people. Now they're doing the opposite extreme by taking the cubes down so people don't feel that suffocation anymore, except now it creates more anxiety, especially for the sensitive, but even the non-sensitive feel it. Most people need regular bouts of privacy. It's not healthy to be sitting on top of people five days a week all day long. You're absorbing the energies at a magnified rate. It also hinders creativity, raises anxiety, decreases productivity, lowers morale, and carries sound. Conversations are louder as it doesn't have the walls to muddle them down, so you hear chaos all day. Most people are working in offices that require your thinking caps. This includes creative people, to technical people, to accountants. You need that private space to focus.

Being in an open office space can be an introvert's nightmare, since that type of personality needs personal space to function well. In fact, studies have shown that productivity goes down when you knock down the cubes. There are more distractions around you and people constantly feel as if they're being watched even if it's not true, so they're on relentless edge, which starts to affect their overall health. It's a catch 22 that people still can't figure out what to do, so they do what's trendy at that time in history.

People complained about cubicles being a prison, but then when the cubicles got knocked down, those same people realized that in hindsight the cubicles were a luxury. The open floor plan is just a bigger prison with more people in it. People spend most of their lives at a job. They certainly don't want to spend that same amount of time staring at people five feet away from them all day around the clock indefinitely for years. Studies showed that the cubicle increased productivity, gave employees their own personal space, which equates to feeling more comfortable and freer. This all translates to a higher morale and stronger productivity. You need the cube to think clearly with fewer distractions. Taking down cubicles makes the office louder, which can distract other colleagues. It also increases stress due to the lack of privacy. This doesn't mean privacy to being up to no good all day long, but having people gaze off into a hypnotic stare at you from afar while you work is uncomfortable. While some people may not have a problem with the openness, they will have an issue with the noise level.

There wasn't one person that I communicated with who let me know that they loved the open office set up. Every single person had some negative thing to say about it. There is a time for productivity and a time for getting work done. Some have complained that they cannot have a business phone conversation in an open office, so they take it outside or in the lobby of their building. If that's the case, then why not just work from home. Others admitted to being able to get more work done in a cubicle or private office. This was because they could balance that with taking mini-breaks to re-adjust their focus with mind enhancing games to conversing with colleagues.

Imagine working in an open office space, then two people chat, followed by another joining in, then suddenly people from across the room are listening and shouting out in harmony. There is one person trying to focus on something important and they're unable to. Suddenly no one is getting any work down. The open office doesn't work for creativity where focus and analytical probing are essential. While the more extroverted personalities might prefer an open floor plan, the majority of people prefer some measure of privacy. It's basic human nature to desire your own private space throughout each day. It's not healthy to spend nine hours a day in an open office sitting on top of other energies, especially if one or more of those energies is toxic. The open office set up works if people are spread out and there are only a small amount of employees, otherwise it's got a chaotic frenetic feeling.

The flip side is that the open office space trend is contributing to the rise to another trend, the working from home trend discussed in an earlier chapter. Eventually companies will be splitting the employees time between working from home to working in the office the other half of the time, pending they work a job that can be done from anywhere. Since most jobs post 2000's are technical related jobs, the answer is it is more likely they can indeed work from home.

One guy I asked about the open floor plan jokingly said, "You can't even pick your nose in peace." One said, "You're basically exposed all day long and it's uncomfortable." Another said, "It feels like a chore to put on the happy face. Every single time you walk in you're assaulted and bombarded by those around you alerted to who is coming in."

While one girl said, "You have to engage in unnecessary gabbing in an open office space even on days when you're not in the mood. You just arrived and need to immediately get into something important that is work related, but you can't because you're forced to have to put on the fake smile and have mindless chit-chat with everyone who is alerted to your arrival."

It's true that it can be impossible to put on that happy sociable smiling mood in front of all those people day in and day out indefinitely for years every second. You can't retreat to your private space if you just want to work quietly and go home on one of the days. You have to be turned 'on' every second. It also delays you into getting to work on matters that need immediate attention.

A small percentage may like the open office floor plan as they could engage with others better. However, in my research I found that there was no improvement in engaging with others that way as opposed to just walking over to their office or cube to engage. The majority of people who liked the open office environment all have their own private offices, so what does that tell you?

You work hard on yourself to grow spiritually, but it's super challenging to keep that consistent when you're working in a toxic work environment that defies that. You don't know what to do about it. I understand because I have also worked in environments in my former work life where the boss or an employee was toxic. There is always that one rotten apple in the bunch that you can't stand or relate to who comes off more antagonistic to you than anything else. They have not been trained how to appropriately behave in certain situations. I've worked with challenging disconnected superiors in the past as well.

You're trying to work on yourself and your soul on a spiritual level, but at the same time you live in the physical world with physical world demands and people who operate primarily from the darkness of ego. You have bills to pay and need to survive, so you can't just quit and hope for the best. You still have to be responsible in order to endure life on Earth.

It's one thing to have to work with a toxic colleague, but a toxic superior is ten times worse than that, because you feel powerless due to being a subordinate to their position. It makes you feel even more like a subservient. No one should have to put up with any kind of abuse, especially in venues that are beyond your control such as the workplace. To a larger extent, you can control who you engage with in your personal life, but the workplace is where the greatest discord is because people can't necessarily choose the employees that are part of the company they work at. They most definitely cannot control the bosses they end up with, but you can control how you choose to deal with it.

The physical life is not without its roadblocks and discord. You didn't ask to be put in a workplace situation with a toxic boss who is completely oblivious and unaware. Enlightened ones and evolving beings know what they're up against by agreeing to incarnate into an Earthly life. This doesn't make it any easier, but having some measure of reality in check as to the balance you're required to partake in to physically survive is essential.

CORD CUTTING AND SHIELDING

Anytime you leave your home and venture out into the world where running into someone is likely, then visualize a shield of protective white light around you. Imagine this shield growing stronger and brighter, especially if someone toxic is communicating with you. Call in Archangel Michael and ask that he surround you with white light. You can call in any higher being of light, from your angels, your spirit team, your guides, Jesus, and so on. You can also go directly to source and call in God. Calling in your team is also calling in God since higher beings of light are extensions of God and a part of Him.

"Archangel Michael, I call upon you now, please surround and shield me with bright white protective light. And it is done."

The shield of light begins to fade and disappear by the next day, so this is something that will need to be done daily. The wear and tear of life and toxins that contaminate your aura will beat itself on this light cutting into it, but having this light around you is stronger than not having it around you. This isn't some new age ridiculousness. This is something I've been doing for most of my life where I've run tests by watching what happens when I shield or don't shield. I've noticed distinctively large differences between having it and not having it. When I did not have it, the day was harder and more challenging than the days when I do have it.

When you come into contact with someone who behaves in a negative, toxic, or antagonistic way with you or around you, then immediately call in Archangel Michael and say, *"Please cut the cords between myself and (the person's name here)."*

You can mentally say while that person is talking to you, *"Please also remove this person from my vicinity as fast as possible."*

Shield and cut the cords to anyone or anything that is toxic in your life. A cord is an etheric energy cord that clairvoyantly looks like a gasoline hose latched onto you with the other end being latched onto someone or something else.

I've cut cords to irritants daily and began to notice that a positive shift would soon happen. The shifts would include where I'm moved into a better place, the other person is suddenly more tolerable, or the extreme is they were laid off or even fired. I don't choose what I want to happen to them since that is outlining. I leave that up to Heaven to handle once I've made the formal request. You have to cut cords to the toxic person daily and never stop until you see that positive movement has been made in the area of concern.

In the morning, make it one of your rituals to mentally call in the Archangel Michael. I tend to light a Sage leaf, which you can do or not. I allow the smoke to envelop and cleanse me, *"Archangel Michael, I call upon you now. Thank you for clearing my body and soul of any negativity or toxins absorbed. Please cut the cords between myself and (name of toxic person in your life here)."*

You don't have to say it accurately or perfectly. Saying it in some manner is key. You have to ask for help in order for the intervening to happen. I'm sharing this because it's worked for me, otherwise I wouldn't feed anyone anything that hasn't revealed improvements for myself first. I try the stuff out, immerse myself fully integrating in it, and then I share whether or not it was effective.

Sometimes the shifts and changes were immediately witnessed after the cord cutting exercise, other times it was gradually over time. The changes soon shifted eventually whenever I would conduct this cord cutting exercise. When I didn't cut the cords, then I noticed the contaminated environment or toxic individual persisted indefinitely.

Some of the changes that took place is the situation would improve with that person or our connection developed positively by becoming a healthier dynamic. The other changes in some cases were they were removed from my life in some way or I was guided and moved to an upgraded environment. I've had numerous readers of mine reach out after learning about this cord-cutting task. They would say with grateful surprise, *"This is weird, it actually worked!"*

Another action step to take to resolve a toxic work situation is to look for another job on the side or keep your eyes open to other means of work. Of course, that's not a guarantee that you can be drama free. You could end up in another work environment with another similar boss or situation far worse than the current one. It's a 50/50 chance that it will end up that way. The other 50% chance is that you end up in a much better situation than you are currently in.

Ask for Divine assistance to help in finding a better job with a more peace loving compassionate boss, employees, and environment. If that's not possible or another job isn't forthcoming, you will still need to acquire additional action steps to at least alleviate the issue somewhat, otherwise it will continue.

There are a myriad of steps one can take that won't necessarily correct the situation as it's up to the boss or the culprit to correct it. It may require you having to come out of your comfort zone and defend yourself before it gets to the breaking point. You can be assertive about requiring compassionate respect.

As mentioned, I've had to confront past superiors and employees who were out of line and disrespectful. After I've done that, there was a shift where we became friendlier with one another. In truth, they hadn't realized they were coming off that way.

There will be instances where that is not the case, and saying something doesn't go well. The other person may become defensive. However, more often than not, I have witnessed a shift in the other person where it's acknowledged. They gradually do their best to change little by little or as much as possible. You have to teach some people to be respectful. I know there have been situations where I was unaware that I was the antagonist, but I took steps to be more mindful of it so others didn't feel uncomfortable. I know I can come off intense and strong, which at times has scared others who didn't know me well. Sometimes it's as simple as mentioning it to the person.

There are other possible ways to deal with inappropriate toxic people in the workplace. Calling them out on it doesn't necessarily mean in an aggressive manner, but firmly and calmly letting them know their rudeness isn't necessary or appropriate. I know that could be a dangerous thing to do depending on who you're dealing with. It could go an entirely different way where the abuse gets worse or you get fired for insubordination. When I've lashed out it's because I don't have a filter or restraint. I fight back and either I've been lucky that nothing bad has come of it, or they realized how intensely I demand that others communicate to one another with respect, even if you are the boss. I've never personally been fired for defending myself, but it's understood that some companies around the world may retaliate.

Some states or countries have been adding additional protective harassment laws. This is where someone could say the wrong thing without intending to, and then it results in a lawsuit or dismissal. If you have a Human Resources Director, then that would be the first place to go. Usually Human Resource Directors don't divulge who reported the person, as it is part of their job to keep it safely anonymous.

A great human resource person is an excellent mediator and will take a complaint seriously wanting to correct the situation as quickly as possible. This is because the human resource person is following and protecting the work state or country law. They know a lawsuit against the company by an employee can create irreparable damage including financial loss.

Back in the day with one of my former jobs, I worked for someone who tended to lose it on occasion. It never personally fazed me, but it did bother other employees, which was when I started to pay attention. One of the employees went to Human Resources. Human Resources spoke to my boss. My boss mentioned it to me at one point. He said that someone in one of his meetings complained to Human Resources about his behavior. He then asked me if he was that bad, and that he didn't realize it, and he'll work on it.

Sometimes it does resolve itself easier than someone might believe, but unless your boss knows this is an issue, they can't correct it. Some people need to be trained and taught how to behave. You have to train people to respect you, including your boss or other employees. Nine times out of ten they're usually unaware of how horrible they are until someone points it out. There have been cases where I have heard others say that you should film or audio record someone losing it and play it back to them so they can get an eye opener view over how horrible they are. That usually buttons them right up. It's like holding up a mirror to someone that is oblivious to their own bad behavior.

This world is growingly transparent than ever before thanks to technology and social media. People have been losing their jobs and careers over being accused of some kind of harassment or recorded tirade. More and more people are stepping forward to stop this kind of behavior. Technology does not hide anything anymore. If someone behaves badly, then it could get out there publicly in a supremely embarrassing way that can ruin someone. This is one of the positives of the technological age, and that is you better button up and start respecting people, because if it gets out into the world that you're a bully with people, the public will not take that lightly. The flipside is that shouldn't necessarily warrant retaliation or firing, since each case would need to be appropriately and objectively studied.

The following recap list on the remaining pages of this chapter are suggested action steps to consider if you're continuing to function at a job you despise:
• Quit.
• Find another job, and then quit.
• Shield daily.
• Cord cut daily.
• Pray daily.
• Tell the suspect using calm assertiveness that the behavior needs to change.
• Discuss it with your human resource director or boss.
• Discuss it with fellow employees you discover are experiencing the same issue. Social support is a nice boost to help you get through it. This is by finding a colleague on the same page as you who feels the same way as you. It helps to have that ally and support so that you feel less alone and isolated about it. You just want to be sure you both don't become buried underneath an avalanche of gossip, since that can be toxic and exhausting on both of your well-being states in the end.
• See the boss's point of view. Discover what is upsetting them and how to positively counter that.
• Keep a private diary or notes on when offending instances happen and file it away should a legal case down the line need to be formed.
• Reach out to upbeat positive friends and support to distract your mind.
• Discuss it with a professional counselor, therapist, or healer.
• Consider natural alternative herbs and amino acids to keep your anxiety or depression symptoms that arise on a calmer level during work hours.
• Talk to your doctor about healthy alternatives if you're not interested in prescribed medication. You can also talk to a professional alternative herbalist.

Some mood uplifting herbs that have positive benefits for people with mood disorders, depression, or anxiety include St. John's Wort, 5HTP, SAMe, and/or Holy Basil. Everyone's body and brain chemistry is different from one another, so what might work for someone else, may or may not work for you. Do a thorough investigation of each herb alternative to see if it will benefit you or not.

And as always, talk to your Doctor before taking anything you don't know enough about firsthand. These are suggestions to investigate on and should not be taken as tried and true methods.

In the meantime, make sure you shield yourself every morning, and cut the cords between yourself and anyone toxic in your life. Do it a few times a day if an issue with someone persists.

CHAPTER EIGHT

Keeping Professional and Personal Life Separate

T reat everyone exactly the same regardless of who they are. One of the reasons I connected with so many in the entertainment business world and formed strong friendships is because of how I interacted with every single person. Everyone was treated equally the same across the board regardless of their job position. This is from the movie star, to the director, to the producers, to the studio heads, to the craft service guy, to the production assistant, to the janitor, and so on. There was no special treatment or behavior change in me depending on who was I interacting with. I remained professional, yet friendly and down to earth with each and every one of them.

When I've witnessed someone kiss the behind of the

higher ups, but be disrespectful or out of line with anyone who wasn't a superior or well known, then this shows you their overall character, which is not pleasant. It can make you cringe or narrow your eyes whenever you see someone automatically alter their personality depending on who they are talking to.

When you are working at a job, then that means you were hired to specifically perform those duties required while at that job. This means who you are outside of that in your personal life should be reduced to the bare minimum. Check your core values at the door, otherwise you will run into some friction that will begin to wear you down. When you were hired to do a specific job, you agreed to do that job. In one sense, this is much like a gifted actor taking on the role of a character they agreed to play on screen or stage, even though they may personally not condone or agree with the characters behavior.

There are cases where ones personal values conflict with the job they were required and hired to do. Kim Davis, a clerk in Kentucky, rose to public attention when she refused to grant a same sex marriage license to a same sex couple. The reasons were because it went against her personal religious beliefs. She ended up being temporarily jailed as a result because the law at the time in Kentucky states that it is legal for a same sex couple to be married.

This is an excellent case example where someone's personal values were so great that it made it impossible for them to the job they were hired to do. Her job was to uphold the law and she broke that vow. When your personal values are so stringent and rigid to the point you won't perform the tasks you were hired to do, then you are no longer qualified to do that job.

When you are hired to do a job, there will be moments where you have to grin and bear it so to speak. Going back to the record store days when I was a teenager, I was helping people from all walks of life. It did not matter to me what they're personal values or choices were as long as they were respectful. I had my personal belief systems and values outside of work, but I never put that upon anyone I assisted. I have no issue with what someone believes in as long as they're not pushing anyone down or hurting them as a result. This goes back to one of the spiritual laws, which is to be respectful and have compassion.

One friend said to me when I was in my twenties, "You have some strict values and ways, but you've never put that on anyone around you or expected that in return. It's really just with your stuff and your own personal environment."

You should be able to have your personal beliefs and values while in your place of work pending it's not harming or negatively affecting anyone. When I would walk into any job I have ever had in my entire life, I checked my ego and personal interests at the door. My job is to do this particular job to the best of my abilities. What I do outside of the place of work is my business. If someone is not respectful, then I've talked to them about it.

The Kim Davis reasoning behind refusing to grant a Same Sex Marriage License is that it goes against her religious views. One of the other many questions I've received from others is what is God's view on homosexuality, since it grew to become a prominent issue in the media. The answer is always the same. All in Heaven are happy to see two souls sharing a committed holy love bond for both of their lives regardless of the genders involved. Spirit does not support or back the information being fed to those who believe otherwise. Every soul is granted free will choice to believe what they want to believe, even if it isn't true.

The mantra I have always had since I was seventeen on my first day on the job was to keep my work and personal life separate. I hold a high value of dignity and presentation in work environments. Past colleagues have described me as independent and focused on the job without ever suggesting or hinting anything revealing about my personal life. I know this might come off like a resume, bio, or as if I'm being interviewed for a job position. The point of illustrating what they thought about me is once again not for bragging purposes, but to demonstrate how I have carried myself with others positively that it benefitted everyone around. It's worked and filtered throughout the company that all began rising to that professional, yet friendly standard.

One producer's assistant on a film I was working on back in the day once said with a smiling revelation, "He has his personal life and his professional life, and they never meet."

I was pleased at how observant and right on the mark she was. It wasn't a criticism, but said with admiration and respect. You check your attitude and personal life at the door of your job. That is a challenge in itself for those who want to have their entire life splayed open to their colleagues from water cooler gossiping to interpersonal friction. Go into work, do your job independently, and then leave work. Rinse and repeat. You don't have to be cold, unless that's your general disposition. You can still be respectful and friendly knowing when to let loose and lighten up, and when to focus on work. Employees need to be able to have fun on occasion. Playtime is not a luxury, but a necessity that is essential to success. When a superior is too much by the book with the rules and instructions, then this wears employees down making them miserable. Yes, everyone has a job to do, but lighten up once in awhile too.

It can be difficult to have this dual life where you have your personal spiritual life you keep to yourself while at work, and this other part of your life where you're spending 30-50 hours a week at a regular practical job with those who don't share your values. You're constantly pushed and tested by those you have no choice in working alongside with. You are required to face and deal with those who don't share your values at this time in your life. Everyone has their own personal separate life outside of work where they are doing things that they also fear they will be judged on. Lead by example as an upstanding employee or boss who remains neutral during the time period you are in a professional environment. Stand by what you love to do outside your work. It's your life and no one owns that part of you, but you.

In past jobs, I always kept my personal life separate from work, but this is also just my personality no matter what I'm doing. I'm extremely private and guarded by nature. Even those close to me never fully know everything. Some may know more than others, but it takes a long time for me to earn someone's trust. There is always an inaccessible wall around me others have pointed out. Those who work hard and prove themselves worthy get as close as possible, but even then some of them have sensed a distance at times.

In popular culture, actress Kim Cattrall made a startling revelation about the nature of her personal relationship with her long running co-star Sarah Jessica Parker in the hit series, "Sex and the City." Fans of the show were surprised to hear Kim say with complete composed poised serious directness, *"We've never been friends. We've been colleagues and in some way, it's a very healthy place to be."*

On screen they played best friends that fans of the show admired and loved, but when the camera's stopped rolling they weren't calling each other, hanging out, or conversing in a friendly way. Many were surprised because the two actors played such convincing best friends on screen.

Those that were surprised forgot to inject the reality that those two actors were working together like any working relationship that anyone has at any job. They were playing fictional characters when the cameras were rolling, but when that part of their job was complete they went their own way.

Many came to Cattrall's defense by examining the realities of their own working relationships and realized they too are similar. They go into work, they're professional and polite with colleagues, perhaps engaging in the occasional idle small talk chit-chat, but when they leave work, then that's the end of it. They're not best buds glued to the hip.

In some rare cases, working relationships may carry into a best friendship. While I have many gained friendships I made while in the workplace, it technically did not catapult into a deeper friendship until after our run with that particular job was complete. There were also those I never heard from again. We had a professional appropriate relationship and when it was over we harmoniously moved on.

CHAPTER NINE

Knowing When to Quit
and When to Move On

Your Spirit team watches and guides you as you move about your Earthly life journey. Some of the ways they communicate to you is by throwing signs or clues on your path to get you to notice. They also communicate with you through your etheric sense channels. Those senses include the four core psychic senses that every soul in existence is made with:

Clairvoyance (clear viewing/seeing)
Claircognizance (clear knowing/thinking)
Clairaudience (clear hearing/audio)
Clairsentience (clear feeling/sensing)

Having psychic abilities are not resorted to a small special group. Some popular known psychics might purport to shout that they're a rare world-renowned psychic medium, but the reality is that all souls are born psychic, including the ones that don't believe in the phenomena.

The creators of "The Simpsons" television show may be personally indifferent to psychic phenomena, yet as viewers have noticed over the years, they have been injecting psychic premonitions into their shows not realizing they are. Things such as predicting Lady Gaga's Super Bowl performance, to Donald Trump's Presidency, to Walt Disney Studios purchasing 20th Century Fox Studios. These were storylines weaved in years before any of those situations took place. This is an example of one foreseeing the future, but not realizing that they are. They thought they were just making it up for a story.

Your Spirit team is dropping in guidance and messages often without you realizing it. They will place these signs and nudges in front of you until you snap to and acknowledge it. Look back on the times in your life when you had a strong sense about something about to happen, where you knew you needed to pay attention to something. This resulted in the premonition coming to fruition. Many will say without realizing they received a psychic hit, "I had a feeling this was going to happen."

Spirit knows your thoughts and how you feel, therefore you can never get away with a lie or deception with them. This is because nothing is hidden from them about you. They know when you're crushed inside, or when you're anxious every time you head into a work environment you're unhappy at. They understand your fear over leaving a job due to not having the finances or security to do so.

When you request their assistance they can guide you towards work that they feel will be more meaningful for you. They can help ease the anxiety experienced in a work set up you're unhappy at. They may reveal an answer that same day or as soon as they're able to help maneuver changes. This is pending that it is part of your soul contract and that it benefits your higher self.

Changes don't always happen immediately. Numerous factors come into play as to why a delay is taking place. One of them is that a request may not benefit your higher self at that time. Another factor may be that they are putting the same idea into your mind to take action on, but you're not following it or you're brushing it off not realizing it's coming from them.

They are also working with another person's Spirit team with the intent of getting a toxic person to make changes that will ultimately benefit you and all involved. Because of this, they are also working with a soul's free will choice as well as someone's lower self. Your lower self comes from the ego, which is not psychic or in tune at all. Your Spirit team may be attempting to work with someone who isn't paying attention to the signs and nudges they're receiving, so this can delay certain events from transpiring.

No one should have to endure a toxic atmosphere wherever they are. Spirit doesn't like to see people struggle in job positions that make them unhappy. It's not like they get joy watching you feel stuck leaving you dejected. They understand this prevents you from contributing positively towards humanity and the planet in some way. You did nothing wrong in attracting that kind of a situation to you necessarily. At the same time some action steps need to be taken on your part. Otherwise a situation will marinate in stagnancy longer that it needs to be.

Nothing is forever and jobs don't last indefinitely, because Earthly life isn't permanent. Even a non-believer in anything outside of the physical world can agree on that. This is why in the end a stagnant situation will not endure for centuries, but you don't want it to permanently bury you underneath an avalanche of despondence.

A growing number of people have been walking away from toxic job situations now more than in the past. There was once a time in history when someone would be hired at a company and they would stay at that company until retirement. Today the average length of time that someone stays at their job in general is three to five years, regardless if they love it or hate it. You're considered indispensable if you've remained at a workplace for any amount longer than that. It looks good on your resume when you've had that kind of longevity. It indicates you have loyalty and that you're trustworthy and likely good at your job if you haven't been let go for poor performance. Potential long-term relationship suitors also see that as a plus as well too.

When someone is looking for a long-term love relationship partner, they may be apt to notice important quality traits in that person's life such as being an asset in their workplace. It shows that you have perseverance and reliability, which can be transferred to the stability of a love relationship. Staying at your job is now considered rare due to the high numbers of people leaving their jobs after only a small handful amount of years.

Times are different where people not only walk away from a job sooner than they used to, but they ironically also walk away from their relationships in a shorter amount of time too! Working things out is not on the agenda list of ones ego. Durability and endurance have been thrown out the window in today's civilization. This points to an even bigger problem that warrants some deeper examination. There are always the pros and cons to most anything. The plus is that people are less likely to stay in a situation that is toxic. The con is that the situation may not actually be toxic, yet you're walking away from it anyway because you're bored with it or it's grown stale.

Has it actually grown stale or are you hopping from one situation to the next every ten days because you're dissatisfied with life overall? Situations will grow stale and boring no matter how exciting it might have been at first. Everything seems exciting in the beginning from a new relationship, a new job, to a home move to a different location. The excitement of that newness will always wear down into stagnancy at some point.

Life is work because you have to work at it to keep it interesting. Find creative ways to inject fun into a situation if it's grown dissatisfying to you. Running away from one set up to the next due to feeling bored with it doesn't fare well with potential employers or personal love suitors. That may not matter to you in the end, but it might when you find as you grow older it becomes harder to run away, and then you discover that your past loyal connections are non-existent.

There are some personalities that need constant stimulation in life or they will grow bored every few weeks. If this is your personality, then seek out jobs where you can easily incorporate the constant stimulation. I worked in the film business for numerous years and one of the things I loved about it is that the film production will eventually end. There is no way for me to grow bored or experience stagnancy because it's always changing. It's like the circus moving from one locale to the next. As a writer, I can do that job from anywhere, so I'm able to pickup and move about to another locale if I need inspiration or stimulation and movement. My relationships and friendships are more than enough stimulation to keep it interesting. According to those close to me, I'm so changeable as it is every hour that they never know what they're going to get. That keeps things interesting and is applied to the longevity of the set up.

Other reasons that push someone to leave a job are

when they feel the position is no longer a perfect match. Some of it is beyond the reasons of toxicity. People leave if they're not feeling challenged enough, if the interest in the work at the company has plateaued, or there is no advancement. They may leave if there is no growth opportunity or the pay increases become infrequent to non-existent. They will leave if they have goals that exceed and surpass the job position. They will also ultimately leave if they work with micromanagers, which is another form of toxic behavior. No one likes to work with a nitpicker for long.

If you're the micromanager, then you hired a person to do a specific job, so let them do the job with minimal interference. Not only will micromanaging someone foster resentment, but it will eventually push them to leave. If they don't leave, they will grow permanently downhearted, which will affect their performance and hurt the company in the process. This will also lower employee morale creating a ripple effect with that energy by spreading it to everything the employee connects and interacts with from other co-workers to the company at large. Oppressive environments and behavior from others does not make anyone leap with glee. It creates a stressful and repressive work atmosphere. This atmosphere is energy that will expand attracting in more of that same downtrodden energy. This negatively affects everything connected to the company.

On a personal level, this will create a block in your life preventing positive abundant opportunities from efficiently moving in. If nothing positive is happening in your life and you feel permanently pessimistic at a job, then that broken feeling is creating a block. That energy inhibits the positive flow of good stuff into your life.

Other things that will create oppression, stress, and resentment are when you consistently push work on an employee after work hours. This negatively inflicts on personal quality time. This goes back to the earlier chapter on incorporating balance into both work and personal life. This means avoiding doing anything company work related during personal off time.

When someone puts work on anybody else after work hours, then this shows that they don't see the employee as a conscious thinking feeling human being. They see them as a number to do with them as they please. Every individual needs to have a personal life that is disconnected from work. This quality personal time off is essential to keep that person operating at full capacity. Time off is both a luxury and a necessity.

Popular culture trained the human mind to see someone working around the clock as something awesome, but it's looking less sexy to the newer generations coming up. If one doesn't have that separate personal life, then they will experience burn out, which affects their quality of work, morale, and overall well-being. It will also harm personal relationships from friendships, to lovers, to family members who seem to say, "I never see you anymore."

That's because you're working a job that has taken over your life preventing you from getting back into the fun of personal time.

When an employee has taken all they can take, expect them to eventually quit sooner than later. Boundaries that are continuously invaded with work around the clock will create resentment, stress, and anger. All of those feelings are not aligned with positive productivity with anything.

I've interviewed hard working professionals that have admitted that when they took that extra day off where no work was thought of, done, or engaged with on any level, that this helped re-charge their batteries with excitement to soon dive right back into work again. This essential personal time off just for you not only helps in recalibrating your soul, but this also has an advantage on your work life. It makes you more excited to get back to work once you've had that personal time to adjust and recharge. When you don't take the time off, your work grows stale and sloppy. Your morale drops hardening your attitude in the process. None of this helps in moving productivity along.

This is your life and you need to live it for you. Allow no one to shatter your dreams, feel no guilt about who you are, and don't apologize about your gifts. It's no one's business how you choose to live your life. You may feel indebted to certain people in your circle this lifetime, but in higher truth the only soul you are beholden to is your own. Live your life freely and go after what you desire with passion, enjoyment, and enthusiasm.

Life may have dealt you a challenging hand, but every soul on the planet is battling with some sort of challenge, even if it's different from yours. Use your challenges to your advantage by turning it around into something good. Challenges are not intended to punish you, but to strengthen and toughen your resolve for a reason.

Don't allow setbacks to hold or keep you down. When you trip, stumble, and fall, then rise back up ready to forge on into battle. Say, "The best is yet to come."

Revert to faith by leaning on God, a higher power, Jesus, the Archangel Michael, or whoever your spirit is personally drawn to for strength and support.

CHAPTER TEN

Working with the Law of Attraction

The law of attraction is an interesting principle because on the one hand being positive around the clock will not automatically equate to positive things falling on your doorstep. Someone might have an overall general happy positive disposition, but they forever struggle in the practical world unable to obtain that lucky break that changes their life for the better.

You might have noticed that a miserable curmudgeon seems to rise up the ranks in the business world attracting bountiful finances to purchase their three mansions and two yachts. This is because the laws of attraction are not a cut and dry method of obtaining what you desire. Each person is a separate study to determine their overall disposition, and then you weigh that against their achievements, desires, and accomplishments.

With that said, having optimism still far supersedes being indefinitely pessimistic. Optimism can and will help attracting good things into your life more swiftly than not. This is because optimism is one of a handful of ingredients to add to what is a recipe for success. Miserable people who have achieved may obtain what they desire, but if one compares that to any personal issues they end up battling with as a result, then the cons may far offset the pros. They can end up battling rapidly failing health, to the loss or absence of a good love partner, to loyal friendships, to witnessing their own downfall in the end.

The law of attraction works to an extent, but one of the numerous factors to take into account is that those who are doing their best to attract what they want may unknowingly stall or reverse the process. This is by vacillating in your mind between knowing you will get what you want, to experiencing fear or doubts that it will never happen. The second you experience fears, worries, or doubts, then you negate the positive attraction and the effects are reversed back in the other direction. This is why it sometimes feels like two steps forward and one step back.

It is highly rare to see someone who is in a perpetual depression state receive consistent blessings. Being in a permanent depressed state around the clock cripples you from working hard and taking endless action steps. One action step is taken with no return and the depressed person gives up and retreats for awhile longer than necessary, which stalls the movement of positive energy that was just started by the one action step. It now moves back down in the other direction until there is consistent action being taken.

It is also highly rare that someone that is continuously angry will receive constant blessings as well. This person will be working so hard around the clock in a rage trying to create some kind of dent that never takes off, thus making them more angry. They will forever be fighting against the wind until that demeanor is shifted and dominated by a more optimistic mindset and detachment to an outcome. The journey is often more important than the destination.

You have to believe you will obtain what you desire more than believing you will not. 60% of the time or more you need to believe that you will obtain your desire. It would need to be more optimism than pessimism.

At the same time, it is more than believing you will get it, but incorporating faith coupled with action are additional essential ingredients to add to the mix. It is not enough to believe you will get something by doing nothing. This is how those seemingly mean people achieve their desires. They believe they will get it and they take action to make it happen. They may be miserable people, but they do believe they will get what they want, and as a result they do get it.

Saying someone is miserable is subjective. They might appear that way, when in fact they are as happy as can be to those close to them. They are simply ambitious, which to some is considered a dirty word that has the stigma of something negative to some folks. Ambition is not a dirty word when it comes to productivity and creativity. This is someone who loves what they do and they keep doing it with a great attitude, hence they start to see blessings coming in as a result of that.

When looking to attract in something you desire, avoid thinking about or entertaining anything associated with fear. Fear that what you want won't happen or that you're not qualified for something. Fear is a dangerous emotion that conjures up and produces so much uproar and upset individually and globally. If you want something, then go out and get it without skepticism or hesitation. When something positive is offered to a pessimist, the pessimist will say, "That's easier said than done." That mindset is a block guaranteeing that it will never happen. If you find your response to something positive is countered with something negative, then work on being aware of that, then shift it into something positive immediately. I have watched many reside in negativity and nothing ever happens for them, while those who have a positive mindset have witnessed good things constantly flowing around them and into their life.

Who said getting what you want was going to be easy? You need to have passion, be a fighter, and a shark to get what you want. When I wanted something, I went after it and I eventually got it. I had zero fear, zero training, zero experience, zero time, zero money, and zero support, but I went after it fearlessly and I eventually got it. Focus in on what you want and work harder than anyone you've come across until you attain your desires, but then keep going. Pull yourself up by your bootstraps and do your best to work hard to get what you want.

This also means incorporating regular breaks, retreats, quiet time, personal time, so that you don't burn out. That burn out feeling can also slow down the attraction business. Take your time and enjoy what you're doing as you move one action step closer towards your goals.

Nothing was ever handed to me. Growing up I'd watch others obtain things effortlessly while I struggled. I knew I had to work for what I wanted or it would not transpire. If I entertained that rare doubt, then what I was focusing on wouldn't happen, or a whirlwind of negative circumstances and delays popped up. This is another hypothesis I've tested out my entire life to ensure it works for me first. I'm unable to stand behind anything I'm not experienced with firsthand.

Something can feel overwhelming where you're left wondering how you're going to go after it, so you don't bother. There's no way you should agree to live like that.

You don't want to be a sitting duck waiting to die metaphorically and literally. Put some fight into your life. I've been plagued by social anxiety and social phobias my entire life, but when I wanted something deeply, I refused to let that stop me. I walked in with those anxieties, and nailed what I wanted with those fears in there. It's kind of like some entertainers before they take the stage to a stadium full of people. They have admitted to being nervous beforehand no matter how good they are at performing, but they suck it up and go out there anyway to do the job they agreed to do.

The Universe and your Spirit team are not going to hand you anything for free. They help those that help themselves. They open doors for those they see are doing their best to put in an effort, regardless if that person is a believer in a higher power or not. This is why you have likely heard or witnessed atheists or non-believers achieve great things. It's because they believed they could and went after it with enormous passion. They are not exempt from success because they're not believers of a higher power. A higher power and spirit beings have no judgment on such things. If they see someone trying to achieve something great, then they will lend them an additional hand regardless of believing in spirit or not.

CHANGING JOBS
AND THE WORK LIFE PERCEPTION

Most people never have the luxury of ever reaching their dream goals in life. They may feel stuck in a job that is not their dream job, but it pays the bills in a world that is forever ripe with unemployment. Be thankful and grateful you have a job that helps pay the bills while doing your best to continue looking at other options. Maybe the odds are against you, but you'll never know unless you try and increase your chances of succeeding by participating.

Even if you obtain the job of your dreams, there will still be imperfections and issues that arise that need to be dealt with and addressed. The most successful highly paid business super stars are not without issues they have to oversee and resolve. You may not be in your dream job, but make the most of it and use it to your advantage to gain additional experience you did not have before you took the job. The longer you're at a company, then the better that looks on your resume.

To one extent, it is easier to find a job when you have a job. This is because you're not stressed out over looking for a job that you'll accept any position offered to you. When you have a steady paycheck coming in, then the burdens to look for another better job are lifted. You can take your time looking for that improved job while you have income coming in. You're more relaxed about the job hunting scenario you've decided to undertake. In the meantime, you're building additional work experience. The flip negative side to that is you may stay at a job you despise fearful of accepting other job offers wondering if it will end up being worse than the one you have now. This is a minor challenge that could go on in your inner mental debate.

Part of networking involves the ability to communicate efficiently. This carries over to being able to get your name out into the job market of your interest without aggravating anyone. It requires the right amount of balanced finesse and tact. Persistence and passion are some of the key ingredients to getting noticed, which I've been successful with both professionally and personally. That last part is said with the objective of illustrating what has positively worked for me time and again over several decades since I was a teenager. Persistence and passion are excellent qualities that anyone of substance finds attractive.

Potential recruits overdo it with their inquiries to the point they turn off the employers. This is because they will consistently bombard the company with daily phone calls and queries. This ends up having the opposite effect of the desired intent that results in the company avoiding you. Use calm assertiveness and reduce the check in queries to once every 4-6 weeks or more. This isn't 4-6 times a week, which has turned off potential employers or people that can help.

Every 4-6 weeks ensures you're not spamming the potential employer, but are popping in once in a blue moon where it's just enough that they start to remember you, but not too much that they become annoyed and turned off by you. Employers are not sitting around doing nothing waiting for your repetitive reach outs. They're often slammed busy with company work chores.

Communication is important to a degree. This is communicating what you desire with your Spirit team, to communicating your name with potential employers. Approach others that can offer guidance or assistance in the areas that appeal to you to work in. This is also by approaching them cautiously, carefully, and with respect. Do your research on the company and the employer you plan to approach so that you have an understanding of their overall nature and personality.

Regardless if you're happy or unhappy at your current job, consistently keep your resume polished and up to date, even when you don't plan to look for new work anytime soon. This will also make it easy to pull it out at the last minute if needed for any reason. There are cases where someone wasn't looking for work, but one day a headhunter offers them an unexpected dream position.

WORK LIFE THEMES IN ENTERTAINMENT

Avoid using negative words, thoughts, and feelings whenever possible. This includes repetitively using them over your current situation such as consistently crying out, "God, I hate my job!"

Okay, you hate your job, but what can you do about it? If you say, "Nothing, I'm just stuck." Then you may as well do the best you can to get over that you hate it. If that's impossible, then at least try to shift that hate to something you want like, "God, I wish I could find a better job!" That's certainly a step above, "I hate my job."

Complaining daily about your job doesn't help change it. You're just endlessly complaining about it annoying everyone around you, and perhaps even yourself if those are the only thoughts you have everyday. It certainly doesn't help in the law of attraction process. When a successful entrepreneur doesn't like something, they don't spend days complaining about it, but instead they seek out potential action steps they can take to fix it.

It's already understood by the working class that many people are in jobs that don't give them pleasure, but a paycheck. They do what they can to keep going. This has inspired many popular artists and singers to write numerous songs in entertainment about it. These are tunes about looking forward to Friday night.

Bruce Springsteen seemed to cover these themes quite a bit in his career. He grew up in that world and environment and so he understands it well. As an artist, you write what you know. Some of his songs were about the hard working lifestyle of living for the weekend with tunes such as, *Working On the Highway* or *Downbound Train* from his *Born in the U.S.A.* album in 1984, as well as *Out on the Street* from *The River* album in 1980 with lyrics such as: *"And Monday when the foreman calls time, I've already got Friday on my mind."*

Many of his songs have spoken about or to the working class crew that drudge it in long hour day jobs that paid the bills, but which were not that person's passion. Those jobs were merely a paycheck to survive, but which take up most of that persons time ultimately making them depressed, exhausted, burned out, stressed, and miserable all around.

How about Donna Summer's, *She Works Hard for the Money*, which came out in 1983? It was a song allegedly inspired by an incident where Summer was at a popular restaurant, went into the restroom, and found a female bathroom attendant taking a nap. The woman woke up and apologized to Summer explaining that she works full time at another job before going to that one. She was more or less burned out that she uncontrollably dozed off at this job. This inspired Donna to write a song that ended up becoming one of her biggest hits. The song was about people like this restroom attendant who work so hard in life at a thankless job while being ignored by society. As one of the lyrics states, *"She works hard for the money, so you better treat her right."*

You will notice that a great deal of entertainment in music and films that focused on work life themes started to rise up in the 1980's and beyond, along with the 9 to 5 film mentioned earlier. This indicates a forever growing issue surrounding humanity's unbalanced work lives. It's been a big deal that it's been brought to light to address numerous times for evaluation and enlightenment through popular culture. This is one of the many ways that Spirit infuses important messages to the masses, by inspiring popular artists to address it in their work. They reach more people that way. Unsurprisingly, many of these pieces end up being successful because so many people around the globe can relate to it.

Country music has also been a place of venting the

frustrations of working in a toxic workplace with no incoming abundance in sight. One of those infamous tunes was, *Take This Job and Shove It*, written by David Allen Coe in 1977 and becoming a huge hit sung by Johnny Paycheck. It's a song that had crossover appeal where all working audiences could relate to it.

Eventually songs were produced about looking forward to the weekend instead of Friday night, because as work hours grew increasingly longer, people have been either working late on Friday's or have been too exhausted from the work week to have enough extra energy to go out. Instead they collapse on the floor by 8:00 pm with a bowl of cereal. The more rebellious will have a glass of wine, beer, or more, and then collapse on the floor.

There was also the hit show, *Roseanne* created by stand up comic, Roseanne Barr. The show broke records and toppled the ratings in the late 1980's and early 1990's. It was one of the few accurate portrayals of the American working class family that also added humor to their struggles. It was no surprise that the Television series that circled the Conner family ended up shooting to #1. It later became a long beloved classic that has been well loved by fans for decades long after it went off the air. In fact, it was so popular that it spawned a successful revival of the show in 2018, over twenty years after it was off the air.

The newer Roseanne episodes produced decades later continued its theme of looking at the trials and tribulations that the American working class struggles through. The fictional children to Roseanne and Dan Conner were grown up and in their forties in the later episodes, but still struggling to find meaningful work as so many are today. It's rare that television shows will accurately depict what people are going through. Generally, entertainment films and television shows will exaggerate the plot lines by giving twenty-something year old characters high end jobs with high end lifestyles, which is an inaccurate depiction of the mass majority and what many people endure in reality.

The new season of the show ended up breaking some records by hitting #1 more than twenty-years later. It was the #1 show on Television and the #1 show for the ABC Network in about twenty-years. This success points to the theme of the show being relatable, many struggling people could relate to it, and it was done well.

This ongoing work life theme of concern has hit close to home in so many ways. I grew up in a household like that. During my work history life, I had to get tough and strict about how I would work certain jobs where I could. As mentioned before, this included refusing to work more than twelve hours during the film production days. Granted, I'm sure some might have thought I was arrogant, but I asked for it and it was approved. The employers on those gigs did not have to comply. They could have not offered me the job or said no to the requests.

I've also interviewed for jobs where I requested to have Friday's off where I would use that day for my writing work. This was during the days when I was attempting to make the transition into an author. All of these requests were permitted and allowed for me to do by the employer. Again, those employers could have denied that request or refused to hire me as a result, but they agreed they were fine with those terms. This is not saying that this is what everyone should do, or who do I think I am, or was. I have always been running my life as a strict disciplined executive ensuring I'm taken care of before I can take care of anyone else, including an employer. They all knew that I would give my 110% during the times I was under their employment and I never failed at that, but instead was rapidly promoted and praised.

I remember one colleague had explained when they

were having issues with staff and the work load, but that when it came to me they added that I may have had Friday's off, "But when he is here, he is here religiously and he has literally been the one that takes care of more than I've seen anyone do while at the company."

Work hard when you work, but work smart, meaning you're not working around the clock. You're doing more in little time, so that the extra time you do have you apply it to personal quality time.

CHAPTER ELEVEN

Partaking in Work That Pleases

Some believe that if you're given a gift, a particular talent, or a divinely inspired idea, then you should give it away without charging money for it. There's the romanticized old view of the starving artist pining away in a tin can, which is absurdly unrealistic. In today's age, unless you were born into money or you're living off a large trust fund, then if you want to survive you'll need to work to make money. You have to charge for your gifts and services, not out of greed, but so you can pay for rent, food, and clothing. When those basic necessities are taken care of, then you're able to focus on what you love without worry or concern of survival.

If you gave everything away for free, then you couldn't

survive. You would have to find a super uncreative full time job on the side to pay your bills, but that could sap your creative energy and life force anyway.

There was a time when people would barter and do a trade with someone, but now necessities cost money. This is why spiritual teachers charge. The only spiritual teachers who don't charge are those who work in a church, but those are non-profit companies where they are receiving donations from members of the congregation to stay afloat. If they didn't receive donations, they would close up, and many of them have. That money goes into their paychecks and the upkeep of the church, so even they are charging essentially.

There are a great many talented healers and artists contributing positive work and efforts towards humanity and their life purpose, but sadly many of them are stuck in regular day jobs that suck up their time and energy. This makes it challenging to pursue their true passion and make a decent living out of it. What makes that feeling worse is that an enormous amount of these day jobs lower their morale. This is because those jobs are bathed in toxic energy in one person or more around them that are disconnected from spirit and the bigger universal picture. If that's not the case and all are a pleasure to be around, the lowered morale can come from your lengthy commute to the job, or because the job is not your passion. That alone can be the reason for the lowered morale. As a sensitive this can be exceptionally taxing on your system, but this is wearing on anyone regardless if they are in tune or not. Being aware of what's greater than your physical body makes it more depressing to be in Earthly set ups that bring you permanently down.

If you're in this kind of a situation, then you are aware that a high percentage of your time is connected to this day job on some level even when you're not at work. This can stall a talented person from working towards what they want to do with their life in the long run. They soon give up and lose faith believing that the Universe is working against them and that they're just not as lucky in the way that others are. Don't give up on the account of someone else. It can be tough at times, but you have to keep going and fighting to do what you truly desire.

One guy informed me that when he's not at work he's sometimes having dreams at night that involves his place of employment or about his colleagues. It didn't start off that way, but when the feeling of wanting to do what he loved grew, then his hatred for his day job grew, which started to manifest into his dreams. This job is embedded deeply into his consciousness. When you're asleep and having dreams about your job, then that's a problem. Your energy is too mired and infiltrated into something that doesn't mean that much to you in the end. You're not at work and you're still thinking about it! It's not even a job he likes all that much, but he's always there which means there isn't enough balance of personal and professional time. Most of his days are spent at his job. This is not entirely his fault as that's the way the current break-your-back mentality mindset of human physical life is at this time.

Find meaningful work at a place that excites you. Consider the steps you can take today to change this whether that be through job hunting or home/apartment hunting. Imagine how many years you can endure in your current state before your spirit is permanently crushed. Working with a weaker boss can add more frustration and stress.

A weak boss asks, "How did this happen?"
A strong boss asks, "How do we fix this?"
This is because the strong boss is interested in moving things forward. The weak boss asks how something happened to stall forward movement and to place blame, which doesn't improve momentum or morale.
"How do we fix this?" is someone looking to keep things going. They have the desire to get others to think outside the box and provide solutions to quickly remedy an issue without wasting any additional time on it. This is the same thought process to have in all of your dealings in life from your daily choices, to your love and friendship connections.

Most jobs require you to be in the office full time, which is currently set to "five days a week – eight hours a day". This varies depending on what city or country you reside in. This time you devote to your job doesn't include the getting ready for work, and driving to and from your place of employment, or your mid-day hour break, which I've discovered many rarely take.
This is also connected to the break your back work mentality that egotistical human beings designed. They had no concept of balance when they set it up that way. No one is happy about it, and bosses and superiors are unaware of it or don't care. Part of that is because they choose their own hours where they may work from home for a few hours before going into the office, or they take their time going in. They receive a larger compensation for the work. When you get paid super well, then you're more gung ho about your job. This is up to a point since those who have larger dreams of doing work they love will do it for free if they had all the time and energy in the world.
I've never personally witnessed a boss or superior who

was working the full 9-6 set up. They've more often than not gone into the office in the late morning or afternoon. One could say they own the company and they can do whatever they like, yet the imbalance is where the employee is expected to be there at the crack peak of rush hour height, and staying until the end of their shift. You know they don't like it, because you've likely noticed how on the dot that employee leaves when their shift is over. This shows they cannot wait to get out of there. If there were more flexibility and trust, the employee would love being there, but the rigid attitude of watching employees like a hawk doesn't leave much room for inspiration or a raised morale.

Some crave human interaction and social stimulation more than others, while other people prefer to function alone. When you have a strong connection with God and Spirit, then you never feel lonely. Loneliness is ultimately longing for a connection to fulfill you that can only truly be satisfied by God. To have a mutually reciprocated blissful love union with another person is to know God, because ones best qualities are parts of Him. Since it's sometimes difficult for a human soul to have a connection with God, the ego part of one's self will crave love, attention, and admiration from other people. It's temporarily fulfilling because no one can ever fill that space within you except God.

All souls desire some form of companionship with at least one person. Some people might disagree, but they do crave some form of a relationship based in love if even through a social circle of friends.

A businessman might say that he only cares about work and money, yet he is cut off from the Universe and the Divine. If he didn't have to get it from some source connected to another person, then he wouldn't crave it at all. He needs other people around him. If all people were taken away from him so that he could be completely alone, then it wouldn't be long before he begins to go crazy and start to miss that stimulation and craving of attention from another person.

In the films, *Passengers* and *Cast Away*, both show one person functioning alone for a long period of time, and eventually starting to go a little mad due to not having another person to engage with at some point.

If this businessman showed up on Earth to find no other people, then he wouldn't know what he was missing. Because there is no material distraction, he would be more in tune to the Heavens unable to hear anything else. This is how human beings progressed in the beginning of civilization. They paid attention to the Heavens and their Divine senses to guide them on how to naturally progress.

Eventually it expanded and exploded to the point of never ending distractions. The more this chaos rose up, the less Divinely connected human beings became. There is no way to escape that and not be aware that it's happening, even if you live in the middle of nowhere. While you might be more connected to Spirit in those areas, you lose the connection when you turn your television on, you surf the internet, you read media stories, or you hop on your phone. Now you are no longer spiritually connected. You might be connected to one another through technological devices, but in a distant loveless way. You are not connected to God through those forms.

The entire planet is unsettled making it near impossible to sense the Divine energy that way. Your subconscious is aware of it, even if you're not paying attention to it in the present moment. However, if you're a highly spiritually connected being, then you're versed and readily able to move in and out of the Spirit connection whenever it calls for it.

Your soul's life force dies little by little living a life you're unhappy with. Perhaps you feel emotionally dead as if you don't have much else to give anymore. You've asked for help for years, and became doubtful that it will ever happen at this point. You're waiting, hoping, praying, and taking action for years wondering if a miracle and blessings will reveal itself to you. It can make you doubt, lose faith, and question if there is a God. It sounds like a roller coaster ride of voices competing with one another from your ego to your angels, to your ego, to your angels.

It is not uncommon to feel disconnected from other people when your consciousness is raised. Suddenly human life appears trivial and superficial. You begin to isolate as a result of not feeling like you can connect with people that understand or can relate to you. Do an inventory check of how the months and years to date have gone in your life. Examine your triumphs, your sorrows, your successes, and your challenges. Look at what was lost and what was gained. You'd be surprised to find the hidden blessings you never thought much of until you look back on it. When things are going swimmingly, people don't often notice it as much as they do when things are going horribly wrong. One can take it for granted until you take a moment to ponder on it.

"Okay, my rent gets paid every month, my health is great, and I have a working car that gets me to work."

Look forward to the coming time up ahead with promise and hope. Have faith and believe that it will get better by accepting nothing less than that mindset.

Success comes and goes the way fame comes and goes. One of the best dreams to come true is being able to turn your love and hobby into a financially lucrative career. You are closer than someone else might be because you understand the concept of manifestation and asking for what you want. If you're stressed out at your job regularly, is the job really worth it? Make wise choices in your life that do not result in leaving you in a bind where you're perpetually unhappy. Take a job for less pay, live beneath your means, until you find the work that makes you feel bliss again.

Looking to the future with optimism you might sometimes find you've been chasing rainbows that evaporate as quickly as the champagne fizzles in your glass. You need not search long and hard for some measure of magic to reveal itself since it's always resided within you. You are loved even when you doubt it, avoid it, shun it and do everything in your power to deny it. When you reach that threshold of completing your Earthly run, the only thing you take with you is love. If you gain anything while here, then remember to love more, give more, and have compassion no matter how unpopular it is. Only then can you truly discover that magic you secretly desire.

CHAPTER TWELVE

Abundance, Money, and Productivity

Every life moves up and down through a series of chapters. When you begin each chapter it is as if you are giving birth to a brand new start with a clean slate that should be accompanied with a fresh optimism and outlook, all of which are essential ingredients to manifesting abundance. Abundance is a word that gets flown around all over the place predominately in spiritual and religious circles, even though most people are aware of what that means. This has made the genre somewhat intoxicating because everyone wants to live a life full of abundance, even if they don't use that word.

A guru uses the word "abundance" and you grow interested and enticed because you feel you're in a position where abundance doesn't seem to be present. People are attracted to money and finances for the benefits that it can offer and assist with. This is a physical world and like it or not, spiritual or not, it takes money to make certain things happen.

Some have called the rich and wealthy derogatory terms like snobby. Not all rich people have that air about them, in fact many successful financially well off people don't appear rich or snobby. They are often the guy with the jeans, t-shirt, and flip-flops. A look that might give the delusion they are a slacker, but then you find out he's the multi-millionaire genius that created a successful start up company.

There are the wealthy folks that are accustomed to a certain lifestyle and merged into that personality where they purchase whatever they want for however much they want. Imagine having all of the money in the world and how that might alter your personality to a degree. Some say money is the root of evil, but that's because in some circles you're also taught to see money as bad or dirty. When you view money that way, then you create a block from obtaining it. This doesn't mean you're intended to glorify money, but it does mean to accept the reality that money is needed to survive on the planet. Otherwise millions of people all over the world wouldn't remain in jobs that have become unfulfilling to them. Those jobs have become more like a lifelong prison sentence with a coffin waiting in the wings for you to climb into and accept the ultimate fate.

You could be someone that struggles to make ends meet in a job you don't care for. No matter how hard you try to create a dent to improve matters, not much change happens to improve your life. While others experience a domino effect of hard times. No one is exempt from challenges on some level. It's true it can appear that others seem to have it easier, but if you don't know them personally, then you're likely unaware of what they're battling with behind closed doors. I've never come across someone who was on cloud nine every single day.

My social circle is in all economic brackets from the working class to the rich and famous, and every single one of them is battling at least one challenging thing in their day-to-day life. Having endless financial riches isn't going to make other problems go away. Money can help to the degree that it relieves you of added worry of not having enough to be able to pay your bills or do work that you love. When you have more than enough income, and you no longer have to slug it in a job you truly hate, then this gives you a boost of optimism, motivation, and productivity. Deep down your angels know how you really feel and they want to help move you out of stressful situations, since they are not beings that desire to see someone suffer.

There were times when I was living paycheck to paycheck, then I was struggling to find a job. Eventually after much fight and perseverance, I started finding great work, and was making more than enough money to live comfortably without worry, but then there were other issues that would arise. Life is full of issues beyond money that pop up from interpersonal connections, to physical, mental, and/or emotional health issues.

The physical life is challenging to navigate when you're stuck in a physical vessel having to do physical chores day after day with no end in sight. It takes work and discipline to get to that space where you are truly comfortable with your life inside and out. This is where you have been blessed enough to be able to create the life you've always dreamed of. Having those dreams is a great start, so don't let anyone squelch them or tell you they're impossible. I had people tell me I couldn't do certain things, but then I'd do them and suddenly they were silent and speechless. When they were saying I couldn't do certain things, what they really meant was that they couldn't. Usually people are talking about themselves when they say you can't accomplish something. They may look at achieving in a limited way, but that doesn't mean you need to or will. Everything and anything is possible as long as you work hard to achieve it. It's not going to suddenly come crashing through the ceiling. It takes resilience and hard work to achieve a life you desire.

You can buy self-help spiritual books like this one, or oracle and tarot decks, go to a psychic or angel reader, purchase crystals, candles, and incense, and on and on. This doesn't mean that will manifest great things. All of those things can certainly help in some ways by offering empowering tools and information that can inspire you to feel good about where you are at and what's to come. In the end, it is up to you to take those action steps and work hard to reach for what you want. Don't let your life pass you by without putting in an effort and fighting for your life.

Many are aiming and struggling to achieve blissful happiness, which includes building their own personal utopia. Never feel guilty for desiring, aiming, and fighting to be happy.

Why would someone want to live a life of misery? There are a great number of people threaded throughout the planet who enjoy living in misery and maintaining a negative disposition. Just take a look at some of your colleagues, friends, or people you know to determine which ones whose life force is gone. Now they're a miserable cold vessel moving about accepting that this is now their life. It's not what they might have imagined, but they've reached that point of having given up on life.

Social media is an exceptional place to visit if you need

proof of the overall general disposition of people today. In fact, more people than not are hooked on living joyless lives. You might think otherwise, but this is permanently evident if you log onto your social media account and see the diatribe of negativity posted up about how someone hates a politician or a celebrity. This trait is unmistakable whenever you read a news story. Many news pieces are bathed in pessimism or destructive blather intended to entice and rattle rather than inform and educate. News stories come off like unbalanced gossip pieces rather than an objective, neutral, balanced, and emotionally detached reporting of facts.

For those seeking to positively improve their lives and raise their consciousness, they do their best to frequently study up and educate themselves on any genre possible, including the areas they would never dive into. When you want to improve your life, you listen to or read stories from those that achieved success and how they did it. You read inspirational spiritually based books in hopes of getting inspired and motivated as a reminder that you can do it too.

Spiritual growth is achieved when you learn lessons that propel your soul forward. There isn't one main event that assists in your spiritual growth, but numerous mini-events interwoven into your Earthly life. Major events will offer larger growth experiences, but the mini-events are just as important if not more so. The side effect is that you make sounder decisions that help you live a more prosperous and abundant life.

One of the tasks to put into practice is working on altering your perception into a positive mindset. I know that may sound cliché, but the reminder is needed when you stray too far off into negativity. Positivity equates to being a stronger abundance attractor, while reinforcing your connection with your Spirit team.

Living for the Weekend

Put it in your mind that you will obtain what you desire. This is pending that what you desire is not harmful to your well-being or another's. It will be something that is beneficial for your higher self's goal and soul's growth. Nothing should stop you from achieving and positively attracting pending it's not harming yourself or another in the end. Fears, insecurities, or low self-esteem are abundance and success killers. The occasional fears will creep in from time to time, but when that's all that is plaguing your mind daily and dominating your thoughts, then it will take over and do its best to destroy your goal. Don't let negativity take over and drown you.

One way to attract in good stuff is by believing you already have what you want. Even when it seems impossible to enter your life, imagine it's a part of your life now. In your mind, visualize and see what you desire in motion.

Actress Nicole Kidman once said there was a time when her fantasy life was richer than her reality. She dove into working on back-to-back projects because her real life outside of work was less than. Over time, this was reversed where her real life became everything she dreamed of with the house, husband, and family. While those particular things may not be of interest to you, the point was that she escaped into work not realizing these other things outside of that were being moved into position. She worked hard and the rewards she desired soon came.

If you keep falling into a negative mindset, be aware of when that happens and tell yourself, "Okay, I need to adjust the vibration levels of my thinking." Then shift and raise the negative direction of your thoughts.

When you've been wallowing in too much negativity, then that can block good stuff from flowing to you. You fall into despair and frustration when enormous time has passed and your desires haven't manifested into reality. When you look back on the passing time, it seems that nothing much in your life has changed. You feel stagnant as if everything has been indefinitely stuck in the mud. You crave positive change and stimulation, but good stuff ceases to flow in. There isn't anything bad or negative happening in your life, which is a blessing that isn't often appreciated, but there is zero movement with anything at all. This can bring you to feel permanently down. You are not where you thought or envisioned you would be five years prior. This can put a damper on your faith and values as you wonder what you've been doing wrong. You may start to fear that Spirit and Heaven are ignoring you or perhaps the non-movement is truly out of your hands. Consider the possibility that Spirit is diligently working behind the scenes throughout that entire time and have just not had much luck getting things moving for you.

There can be cases where you have been putting in the tireless work with endless action steps, and so there is nothing you did wrong to cause your life to feel forever stationary. There could be other factors at play to consider such as that one.

It took me seven years to get into the film business. I was sixteen when I knew that was going to be my next big move. It wasn't until I turned twenty-three when it worked out in my favor. That's seven years of what felt like stagnancy. What did I do during that time? I got my first regular job at the record store chain when those existed. I simultaneously studied up on the creative side of the film business. I read, I wrote in journals, I experienced life, perfected my resume, made lists of entertainment production companies and contacted them. My general disposition was that I was going to get in and nothing was going to stop me. I said, "I will never stop trying to get in. I will keep doing that until I'm eighty, I don't care."

I had the occasional doubt or frustration with, "This is ridiculous. When is it going to happen?" Those negative moments were rare, because that wasn't my general disposition. 95% of the time I was focused on getting in and was excited about that. I just kept working hard to achieve it until by some sheer force of miracle from above I got in. What are the odds that some top movie star is going to hire some young punk kid with no experience? Slim. There was endless praying and taking action steps on my part until one day I received that surprise call back. In fact, when the call came in I was so stunned that it took me an hour to collect myself before calling back. It seemed too good to be true that I went into a hazy state of shock.

The point of sharing that tidbit of a story was that I was no one in particular without any experience. I had to sell who I was personally in a big way. This captured their attention enough to bring me on. This means that most anybody can do it if they convey passion, persistence, hard work, and a great attitude. After talking to me, the company discovered that underneath the punk rebellious aura that there was a super high intellect that dominated the bosses. This was considered a strength and asset to the company. Use who you are, your personality, and those positive parts of you to showcase to the world. People love authenticity and originality in the end. Those that make big decisions like hiring gravitate towards someone who is different than the norm.

One of the positive benefits to technology today is that people can easily remain in touch via phone, email, web camera, and social media. Before the rise of technology, one didn't have that luxury. Even though you've physically moved away from one another, nothing eclipses sitting next to one another physically in person. That strengthens any relationship over anything else. The technological means are extremely beneficial when the two people are not able to be in close proximity to one another. Even though physical in person connections are #1 with a bullet.

People grow closer with physical in person hangouts. Many people forget this unspoken rule because they've become accustomed to staying in touch through technological means. This is true even though they may physically reside twenty minutes from one another, but rarely see each other. The busy work lives of today have made getting together regularly challenging for some people.

Some insist that you make time for those you care about, and while true to one extent, you wonder if those people that came up with that saying work 50-60 hours plus a week. Many don't work those hours by choice, unless they have no personal life worthy of attention. When you have a life outside of work, then you don't want to be sitting at work around the clock, but will insist on incorporating balance.

If the average person is working full time and has a lengthy tough commute, then they are in work mode that many hours a week. This leaves little time for balance, because the time they do have they're running their errands they didn't have time to do while at work, or their body is worn out from work so they end up "crash course resting". This is the behavior of those who are generally physically active. You can imagine what the state is like for someone who is not physically active. While God and higher beings in Heaven insist on hard work, that means hard work that is done in a short amount of time in order to have an equal amount of play time to raise your vibration and well-being levels.

One of the other positives of technology and the Internet in general is that you have endless research capabilities at your fingertips. You can research and read up on how to advance your career easily online. When I was growing up there was no Internet, so I had to go to the library that housed limited research material, but not limited enough that it didn't help me. This is because I could sit in the library as a late teen studying up on the inner workings of the creative side of the film business, which helped me get my lucky break as they say in the entertainment business. While there is endless access to research on getting into any business today, it's ironically become more difficult due to the huge array of competition. Yet, many filter in and out of their business of choice just as quickly realizing the reality that it isn't for everyone, but a specific type of personality. During pre-internet domination days the few that went out there and did the grunt work to get in increased their chances to getting in.

What you can do before you do anything is change your thoughts and get positive. Look at the bright side of what you have in your life today. Take a second and allow the good stuff to flush through you now.

Getting positive and optimistic isn't about covering up your negative thoughts with phony positive ones. The positive thoughts and feelings need to be authentic and unforced, otherwise it's just a negativity mask in disguise like hiding a cut behind a Band-Aid. Feel the good energy by partaking in fun healthy activities that you know will raise your vibration. Feeling positive thoughts and feelings authentically is experiencing those vibrations inside you. It's okay to feel negative as you're human. Many teachings push for positive thinking, which can stress someone out when they're unable to. This is about shifting repetitive complaints into positive action to help you move forward and onward.

Ask for Heavenly intervention and assistance, then pay attention to the guidance you're expected to take action on, then take action on it. Bring in what you desire by allowing it to flow towards you naturally. You're not chasing your dreams in a panic. You're taking productive action steps based in love and serenity to obtain what you long for. If there's someone you're interested in romantically, then ask them out regardless of your gender.

Regardless of their answer, don't chase or burden them by staying on top of them relentlessly. When it's the right one, it will flow and merge with you naturally and organically. Placing any kind of demands will push it away. The same goes for work related endeavors or anything you have your eyes set on. The serious relationships I've had over the course of my life all transpired without effort. It came to be when I wasn't looking or longing, but when I was content. When I was frustrated or in a negative mindset, then nothing came to pass.

Remove anything and everything that is a mindless distraction from your higher priorities. If you have work to do, action steps you need to take to improve your career, or make something important happen, then get to work. Notice how much time is spent during your day with mindless activities. For so many, the obvious answer is social media surfing.

Social media can become addicting where you find you're posting nonsense, or scrolling and surfing all day long when you know you have work to do. It's one thing to take a mindless break for an hour, but another to spend hours online achieving nothing. It's the ego's way of coaxing you into wasting time.

Other time wasters can include chatting on dating/sex apps with people you rarely ever meet or build a long lasting connection with. Time wasters can also fall into addictions such as food, drugs, sex, and/or alcohol. This isn't the same as getting together with a friend on a Saturday night for a drink. This is about the daily time-wasting activities you devote towards each day, instead of contributing productively with action steps towards your dreams.

Incorporate nature outings into your life at least once a week if not once a day. Many people lead incredibly busy work lives where they're lucky if they hit a nature setting once a month. Others may not even consider going into a nature locale or understand why they should. I remember seeing some comedy film where the character was from the city and ended up in nature complaining. There are city people who find fresh air to be the Devil, which I'm sure is amusing.

Some people might have the luxury of living in a home with a backyard filled with nature, while others need to venture off to a nature locale, but will instead put it off. Weeks have gone by and they have yet to take a walk or exercise in nature, or even around the block. This can be due to procrastination, laziness, or having agoraphobia, which is an unnatural fear that prevents you from venturing outside in public. You're afraid it may induce some kind of panic. If you're in a big city, then this can be exacerbated, since people tend to be less kind in the treatment of others. Human beings were made to live on top of one another since this causes all sorts of anger, stress, and impatience.

Many have expressed to me that they find it surprising that I have social anxiety, but there are exercises I have to do before I head outside or communicate with people I don't know. Readers have reached out to me in sharing their similar stories, so I understand the challenge of having anxiety. I push myself to do it daily no matter what. Take deep breaths in, center yourself, and call in your Spirit team to extricate the fear and get you out there.

Nature is filled with high vibrational spirit beings than any other location in the world. When you stroll through a park on your mental health walk you can feel the stresses lifting off your body. Suddenly a wave of focused energy and clarity opens up and brilliant ideas, feelings, and thoughts reveal themselves to you. This is because nature is a therapeutic setting where the angels and high vibrational spirits are able to effortlessly work on you by raising your vibration. They lower their vibration to meet yours and the psychic connection is made.

When I bike down to the beach I notice the shift and change as soon as I reach the top of the hill where I can see the ocean. A strong sea breeze slams into me and it's like I'm soaring. People in big cities live on top of each other, which is not conducive or beneficial on your health and well-being. You have to work extra hard to find a nature setting with little to no people where you can clear your mind.

New York City is considered the highest populated city in America, which is hard to believe considering it's a small area. They might have a harder time, because even the parks are crowded. Los Angeles has the beaches if you're able to find a little patch of space all to yourself with no people. Try to go at a less than crowded hour of the day if possible.

Crystal clear clarity rises in its visibility when you're in nature. Many people sit in cold corporate like boxes all day and all week, only to go home in a cold travelling box. All of this crushes your soul's life force. It's not a place for creative thinking, which is required by all souls, even the business professionals.

Does your life, job, or career role have you sitting all day? You may be noticing that around 2-2:30-ish in the afternoon when you suddenly feel a wave of fatigue and exhaustion and can't figure out why. When there is no other underlying medical issue, then it can be that your body is releasing melatonin telling you it's time to take a catnap. Unfortunately, many work at jobs where that is impossible, so instead you force yourself awake with caffeine to keep going. It's like the "Clockwork Orange" film where you're forcing your eyes open. I've had people tell me they sleep in their cars on their break. They will find ways to squeeze that mid-day rest in.

Avoid eating your lunch at your desk if you work in an office, unless you plan to get outside afterwards for fresh air and a stroll. Sitting at your desk all day long is horrible on your health, well-being, creativity, and productivity. I've witnessed employees who basically sat at their desk from the time they arrived until they clocked out.

Some believe you should continue to work all through lunch. You don't work yourself or employees into the ground. You take an actual lunch and go outside, get some fresh air, walk around, come back to work refreshed. That is what will boost your energy, productivity, and creativity levels, while lowering stress at the same time. Taking frequent breaks are the law in many areas so that people don't experience this burnout or don't fall into a slave sweatshop mentality.

When you wake up at 730am and proceed to get ready to start your day, then you may not be in bed until around 11 pm that night if you're lucky. That's a super long time to be awake, functioning, and turned "on" all day. It's no wonder everyone is exhausted from students to busy career professionals. You keep pumping yourself up with caffeine to keep going because this current life set up by naïve human beings doesn't allow a true honest midday break to rest and exercise before diving back into work.

When people in the past set things up they never considered the human souls well-being and overall capabilities and limitations. People used to praise someone for being able to work for fifteen hours a day without stopping. There's nothing admirable about that anymore. Now one feels bad for those who don't know how to stop and relax.

To raise your vibration and become a strong abundance attractor, you must be disciplined about what you consume and how you set up your surroundings. Focusing on clean healthy diets as much as possible is great on your health and spiritual connection. All of which gives you more energy to work on the projects that matter. Of course, you can let loose and have fun occasionally going for that Pizza and Beer night, but this is about your overall diet and toxin intake and how that affects your day.

It's challenging for many to change their diets to something cleaner and unprocessed or chemical free, especially if you're a 9-6 Monday thru Friday corporate professional. While it is possible to improve your diet, it can still be challenging. When you are consuming cleaner foods, then your body, mind, and soul notice the difference gradually over time. There are a great many advocates for cleaner foods and diets, but they may not have begun making those changes until after they were successful.

I've noticed and experienced positive changes within and around me when I did my best to consume cleaner foods and drinks. The saying is true that you are what you eat. If you're eating bad foods daily all day long, then you cut off the psychic spiritual connection with the other side. If you don't want to hear God, then eat a whole pizza and some ice cream. You won't pick up on anything from the other side for the rest of the day.

CHAPTER THIRTEEN

Detoxing Your World, Paying Off Debts, and Charity Giving

Many sensitive's shy away or keep away from other people due to the negativity that they often associate with other people. Because they sense every nuance, they absorb the negative energies that people emanate more than other souls do. There are good people you can benefit from as they can with you. When the both of you are positive optimistic go-getters, then there is no telling how far you can both go. You feel inspired by one another, rather than brought down by them if they're a gossip or negative complainer. Being around a "Debby Downer" can depress you, which cripples and stalls movement forward. Focus on quality people to surround yourself with such as those who are mutually supportive, there for you, while also allowing you the required space you need throughout each day as a sensitive.

Eliminating toxic friendships also includes those on your social media page. The world is drama ridden and chaotic enough with all the daily gossip noise from politically hyped chatter to celebrity gossip. You've likely noticed that on those days whenever the latest scandal rises that every other person posts their two cents screaming, whining, and complaining about the target. This does nothing to help anyone. It's toxic energy that fans those flames that are undeserving of attention. It brings you down, it lowers your vibration, it blocks good stuff from coming to you, and it puts a damper on your life. You then carry that out in the world and spread that to whoever you connect with. Those you pass it to then take that energy and spread it around as well. Soon the entire planet has erupted into nonsensical chaos that helps no one at all.

I've watched past acquaintances on social media announce that their wall thread is too plagued with negative energy, therefore they are going to take a break from social media. That's one of the great ways to detox from technology for a bit, but at the same time you shouldn't have to run and hide from your own page.

The great thing about some social media sites in general as previously mentioned is that you can unfriend people if you choose, or unfollow them if you don't want to unfriend them. This way you can keep them in your friends list, but you no longer see their posts. This is beneficial for someone you like, but you can't stand the constant negative posts. I did this myself with dozens of people who were the usual suspects that posted negative posts on the politicians and celebrities they hate everyday all day long.

Living for the Weekend

Personally, I don't care who you dislike as I'm not interested in reading that, but if you want to talk about someone you do like and the positives about them, then that's always welcomed. I don't hate those people posting constant negativity, but it was extremely toxic. I knew I wasn't alone as I was hearing from others telling me the same thing and how everyone seems to be out of control these days. The culprits weren't learning to step away from it and I realized they were never going to learn to distance themselves from gossip and negativity, so I chose to hide their posts. By the time I was done hiding people months later, I had a nice clean uplifting page with people who posted more engaging interesting content that was on the positive side. Letting go of negativity allows room for positivity.

When detoxing from people, social media, you also want to detox from distractions and time wasters. These are distractions that eat up good chunks of your day like wasteful internet and social media surfing, knowing that you have work to do or that you could do.

You might have other distractions such as work or family obligations that seem to eat up your day to the point that you have zero time to devote towards your life purpose or to building your side career. This way you won't have to work full time day jobs you despise anymore. You find a week has gone by and you've donated zero time towards your purpose. Sometimes the ego will have you push that away when realistically you could squeeze in a half hour to an hour that consists of one action step towards your passion and purpose. You'd be surprised as I've been there too. This is where I've made excuses that there isn't any time. After weeks of that, I started to pay more attention to the downtime I did have. Okay, I have forty-five minutes before I need to leave for my dinner, I can squeeze in something important now.

You are deserving of blessings as anyone else. When you are blessed, then this will also allow you to do good stuff for others. There is a difference between hoarding money and spending wisely. Once you're taken care of, then it's easier to freely focus on others who could use your helping hand.

Everyone is born with special gifts from psychic abilities to creative skills. There isn't one person on the planet that doesn't have something extraordinary about them to utilize and contribute towards for the betterment of humanity. At the same time, so many amazing people struggle in low vibrational jobs to pay the bills that they end up pushing their authentic talents down to survive. The angels want to guide them out of that. They will maneuver circumstances to help produce blessings to propel that soul forward. It can take them years or decades to help some people, while it seems others are blessed at an earlier age. Avoid placing a time limit on when blessings can or will happen. It doesn't matter how old you are, as you are not discriminated against from receiving blessings and miracles at any age. This is also pending that what you're asking for help with is beneficial on your spiritual path. God blesses goods that are needed and not necessarily ones that you want.

An older person might feel resentment when they see a twenty-two year old popular well-known entertainer purchase a mansion worth three million along the coast with a magnificent view. This doesn't mean this popular star is any deserving or worthy of excessive material abundance over you. In one sense, it might feel like the luck of the draw, or that the maneuvering your Spirit team has been working on behind the scenes is taking longer than another person. It's super easy to fall into envy and resentment, but you don't want to wallow deeply in that energy as that will block what needs to come in.

The other side of that is you don't know the challenges and tough experiences the popular star is faced with behind closed doors. You may say you don't care, but despite their fat bank account, they could be battling with issues far worse than you could imagine. Some find it difficult to sympathize with anyone who doesn't have money issues, but when you do that then you're placing higher value on money. That person with money is human like anyone else and going through personal experiences you're unaware of. What matters to Heaven is what is in your heart and who you are regardless of what's in your bank account.

Heaven is also dealing with human beings that operate primarily from ego and free will. Your Spirit team could be frequently attempting to get the attention of someone important on Earth that can propel you forward, but that person is not picking up on the guidance. As a result, you suffer longer because the person intended to make an important offer to you that can change your life is not following the hunches periodically put in front of them. It can also be you who isn't noticing the guidance coming in or following it. All of that can create an immense amount of delays. Due to human free will choice consistently getting in the way of conclusive progress, it can create an immense amount of delays to seeing your hard work not reap much reward.

DEBT PAY OFF

Paying off debts is essential to balancing the energy in your life. Struggling to get out of debt can create a damper on things. It can lower your vibration when the stress is so great that it starts to mess with your emotions. Paying off your debts for certain things can be done even if it's a small amount each month.

A good line in the film "Parenthood" was when the Jason Robards character says to his son, *"If they are business people, they'll be happy to be getting something rather than nothing."*

This method will also gradually move you out of debt. Don't use more of your credit than you don't have. If you have a credit card and the credit card company offers to raise your limit, then don't sign up for that. It can trap you by increasing your interest and payments per month. You'll be tempted to buy more than you have. Naturally, this would be common sense, but you understand that so many people end up paying for it dearly. It's easy to go crazy with spending when you are under the impression you have the money. Just because your credit card company may say you have that spending limit, it doesn't mean you have that money. Spend what you know you can easily pay back sooner than later.

If you're trying to build credit or increase your credit score, then save the credit card for smaller purchases such as gas for your car. Pay back more than you've spent. Paying off your credit card in one gigantic lump sum can surprisingly drop your score, so keep an eye on that.

Debt can also be an emotional debt as well where you're obliged to another person that brings you negativity and grief. They offer nothing in the way of positivity and you soon wonder how to extricate them from your life. This can be done through gradual dissolving where you're less available for them over time.

SAVING FOR RETIREMENT

In the end, most people are working to have security, to pay their bills, and live comfortably without fear of never having enough money. It's all about money in the end.

Yet, many people find they are working paycheck to paycheck where most of it goes to their expenses. They find it hard and challenging to save money for a rainy day, let alone for security when they grow older.

Avoid waiting until the last minute to start saving money for retirement. Start as soon as possible even if it's just $5 a week, or whatever dollar conversion is used in the country you're reading this from. Five dollars a week does not sound like a ton of money, but if you start doing that at age 21, then by the time you're 41 you could have $100,000. If you're 44, then you'll have that by age 84. If you put in more or you double that to $10, then you'll have something like $200,000. This is all for putting away just $10 a week. You're also not including the other accounts you might have set up where you add a small amount to that too. This can be your 401K as well if you have one.

You don't think much of it when you're moving through your twenties or thirties, but as you grow older you'll wish you had. In my twenties, I had set up private savings accounts, retirement accounts, stock accounts, and other accounts from former jobs. Life moved on, the years continued forward, and I had forgot about looking into the accounts. When I did, I was astonished at how great the numbers were that accumulated in there. Basically, it was more than enough for a down payment on a home.

When you have this set up in a way where it's automatically transferring or putting the money in the accounts, then you don't have to remember to do it, since you'll likely forget. Because you'll likely forget you later go back to it, as I did, and you'll be thunderstruck to find out how much it grew. You don't fear so much about where you'll be, or what you'll have in terms of security when you reach a certain age. You could be employed your entire life, but then there's that one day when you're laid off, fired, or the company closes up shop. Suddenly you discover it's harder than ever trying to find a job in the new market. Take into account there are new adopted ways of working you hadn't been versed much in over the years because you didn't need to know about it. Perhaps an illness or disorder prevents you from working, or you have trouble finding another job, or any other issue preventing income from coming in. You'll be glad you had been saving a tiny amount on the side weekly that it ends up becoming your saving grace. Don't fret no matter how old you are now. It's never too late to start implementing this strategy today. It doesn't matter if you're twenty or seventy. It's better to start late than to not do it at all.

One security measure is that you want to avoid putting all of your eggs in one basket or one account. If by some force of bad luck something should happen to that account, then you risk losing everything. While this is rare, it does and has happened in the past. On a grand scale this happened to others thanks to Bernard Madoff. Madoff was an investor taking people's savings out of the accounts to shuffle it around. They called it one of the largest Ponzi schemes in history. It's true many rich millionaires lost their money by doing that, but there were also the working class folks who worked paycheck to paycheck whose entire savings was in there. Some people committed suicide as a result. To find that after twenty years of working hard someone ran off with your money and lost it so to speak is devastating.

You can watch the Madoff story in, *The Wizard of Lies* with Robert DeNiro and Michelle Pfeiffer.

Recommended films can convey a certain point that is helpful in ones life. Many therapists do that as a matter of fact. Plus, most people like movies, so it doesn't feel like work to sit through one if it's good. What happened with the Madoff story is rare though, but this is one reason to ensure that you don't put all of your money in one place. Spread it out in different accounts even if it's just $5 a week in a couple of accounts. Something is better than nothing.

Organizing your life also means organizing your finances. Many live paycheck to paycheck, but you can still put away one to five dollars a week for life through investments. You'd be surprised how low of an amount of that a week adds up to a great deal of change in ten to twenty years. Think about your future as soon as possible early on. This isn't common to think about when you're under 30. It's as you move into your thirties and beyond do you later wish you invested earlier. Start as soon as possible even if it's just one dollar a week. There are many investment programs available that can help.

Set up a Money Market account or a special Savings account. If you have the personality where you know you'll start pulling money out of it, then inquire with your bank about a locked account where they don't let you touch it for a set amount of years as it's accruing. This isn't hoarding, but saving for your future. Think about where you'll be in older age when finding a day job becomes harder to come by or if you suddenly hit hard financial times later in life.

There is enough room on the planet for every soul to be contributing positively towards the advancement of humanity where all can live in harmony. The world is hard enough to live on with all of the constant negativity and the darkness of ego running the show. You may feel as if you're alone in contributing your part, but you're not. There are millions of souls also doing their part. Rather than display jealousy or animosity towards those who bring positivity to the world, work on thinking up something positive to say about them. It's easier for the darkness of ego to criticize than to praise. Everyone that contributes positivity helps at least one person out there.

Clearing the clutter in your life is beneficial since it allows you to focus more clearly. As a writer, I will incorporate procrastination techniques where I need to make sure my space is completely clear of clutter before I fall into the zone to write.

When you walk into a messy room you immediately sense the chaos, which makes your thinking more chaotic and unsettled. Clear away the cobwebs and the clutter by boxing up or throwing away items you will never need or look at again. If it has deep sentimental value or attachment and you're not ready to part with it, then box it up and put it in a closet or storage if it doesn't need to be lying around.

Commit to simplicity and keep your surroundings organized and uncluttered. Extricate friendships that you don't consider to be true authentic friendships, but connections you keep around due to a fear of loneliness. If the friendship stresses you out, then it's time to begin distancing yourself from them. Friendships that are true and long lasting will place no demands on you or your time. They understand this and form naturally unfettered.

Detoxing your inner and outer worlds isn't just about detoxing your body of bad foods, drugs, or alcohol. It's more than going on a fast or cleanse. It's also about detoxing every aspect of your life from clearing the clutter in your home and work, to detoxing the people in your life. Do a thorough examination of the people in your world from family to friendships. Who brings you down whenever they come around? Work on eliminating and dissolving those in your life that do nothing, but bring drama and chaos to your world. Even if you don't, eventually the angels will remove people from your life that have fulfilled their purpose or contribute nothing of positive benefit, but stall you from moving forward. Get organized in your life and plan, schedule, and organize your surroundings. When you have a clear space, you have a clear mind. A clear mind helps you get focused while allowing your Spirit team's wisdom, messages, and guidance to come flowing in. This guidance helps bring you one step closer to achieving. There is a fine line between overspending on things you don't need, to buying the occasional gadget or item you would love to have. Buying something for yourself is part of self-care. It's when it moves into constant spending to fill an emotional void that you begin to block the flow of abundance.

DONATING AND GIVING

Other ways of bringing more abundance to you is to look at what you are giving, donating, or putting out in the world. If what you put out into the world is negative or gossip ridden, then that is the energy of what will boomerang right back to you.

Donate to your favorite charity, even if all you can afford to spare is $1 a month. Giving something is better than nothing to keep the flow of abundance moving. However, donating with the motive of wanting something in return is not authentic giving. Also donating towards charities that have negative ulterior motives contribute negative energy as well, so you want to make sure the charity is truly positively beneficial. Most political campaigns to help someone with a candidacy are negatively motivated and considered waste. While helping someone of lesser means on the economic scale to helping a child come out of abuse would fall into the positive contributions on that scale. Jesus Christ would help someone in need on the streets before helping someone get elected into a political office.

Donating something positive can be more than money. It can be the donating of your time to help others in need. Finding ways to positively help others and offering the goodness of your heart goes a long way. The angels see that as giving in the "giving and receiving" equation. When you sit around waiting to receive blessings and miracles, but offer nothing in return for that energy, then you'll be sitting around for a long time.

When you give or donate anything, it must be done without wanting in return. There comes a point when good-hearted people that always give and get nothing in return will start to become resentful. As soon as you move into that bitterness, then you have moved out of the positive energy flow of abundance. It's also a sign that you've created an imbalance by giving too much. Energy is a give and take where there has to be an equal amount flowing back and forth. This doesn't mean you halt giving permanently when nothing good has been forthcoming, but it does ask you to slow it down a bit to prevent you from moving into resentment territory. Pay attention to who you are giving to and where it's needed. It's the same way you pick your battles as to what is a worthier cause that calls for your warrior like energy to change something for the better.

Some people are interested in other causes and charities such as animal cruelty, environmental planet work, to finding cures for diseases and health issues. Giving positively of your time, energy, or money without the need or desire for something in return helps open the gates that will allow a healthy flow of abundance into your world.

Opening the floodgates of abundance requires much more from you than sitting around waiting for it to ring your doorbell. You need to be proactive remembering that making no decision or choice is making a choice. By choosing to be inactive, you have chosen.

TAKING ACTION STEPS

You've done the visualization exercises, the vision boards, the dream boards, while continuously praying and asking for help, yet nothing has moved or been forthcoming. Take a step back for a moment and try to look at any repetitive ideas that have continuously entered your mind about doing something or taking action, yet you've done nothing, not followed it, or made any moves. Those repetitive ideas may be guidance filtering in from above. Your Spirit team has been helping and guiding you trying to get you to notice something important, yet you keep pushing that idea away. They will continue to implant the same action step indefinitely until it's finally taken. It doesn't matter if one week passes or one year. That same action step will be put in front of you. Once you've taken action on that, then they will show you the next step.

Perhaps you have fear about taking that step, or you don't know how you'll do it, or you've already tried that but it didn't work. For whatever reason, that idea is still coming in trying to get you to notice it for a reason. Don't discredit those ideas that require you to take action. Taking action is another key step to opening the floodgates of abundance.

Act on the continuing positive nudges you receive and follow it. Don't allow worry to set in blocking you from moving forward. Avoid inviting in more of that negative worry stuff to you. Some have made a vision board or they've put up empowering images and words to remind them of what they want. This assists in implanting the ideas into your mind, which will help direct the energy towards making something happen. Your goal is to fill your life with positive words and phrases that are aligned with abundance. Affirm only what you desire, not what is lacking.

Maybe the action step is taking you out of your comfort zone and you're afraid of making a drastic move that you know deep down you desperately want to make, but you're fearful of what will or will not come. Trust the continuous guidance your Spirit team is giving you. This is putting your faith and trust in God and the Universe that there is a Divine plan laid out to assist you.

It could be that you were asked to apply for a job you wanted, yet you had already applied to the place a year prior and received no response, yet months or even a year later the job is still on your mind. Many companies are open to people re-applying or re-submitting their resume or credentials every six months. You may have received no response the first time, but the repetitive guidance coming in on it again may be no accident. It is asking you to try again.

This has been true for me, as far with the jobs I've had in the past from the record store to the film business. I was turned down initially or I received no response from them. I tried on several occasions on a later date and received nothing, no response, or a sorry not hiring. I tried again at a much later date and that was when I struck gold. This time I received a response to come in, met with them, and was hired as a result. Imagine if I didn't follow the hunches to try again.

Perhaps you were turned down or you turned them down, but the hunches kept coming in stronger over time, so you try again. It's the trying again when it all comes together.

Sometimes you're supposed to be at a specific job at a time in your life for a reason that might not be understood while it's in motion. You could be gaining skills that you will be utilizing later. Only then, do you realize what it was all for. This goes for relationships of all types from friendships, business, to love as well too.

There are times where you've been psychically blocked or you're not receiving a crystal-clear answer on something, while other times it will slam in a matter of seconds. For those times where nothing is coming in, pray, connect, ask for intervention, signs, messages, and guidance.

Before bed and drifting off to sleep, ask your Spirit team to come into your dreams and communicate with you there. Your ego is asleep and your consciousness rises where you're more open and apt to receiving the content while in a dream state. Ask that they help you remember the dream, because sometimes the dreams can be so vivid, but the second you wake up it's gone and vanished. You want to keep a journal or notepad within reach while asleep so that when you wake up, you can quickly jot down the images you received in the dream as soon as possible before it's gone. Even if it has no meaning to you at that point, jot it down as it could have significance later.

Dreaming is connected to Clairvoyance, which is clear seeing or clear viewing, so the messages that come in require some decoding. Write down everything you remember seeing in the dream even if it was a color. Colors have symbolic meanings as well too! There could be some important clues in your dreams that were planted into your subconscious to help you.

CHAPTER FOURTEEN

Working to Find Meaning In Your Life

Working in a job or career that has deep meaning and fulfillment to you and getting paid for it is something many want to achieve. It can be frustrating when you're an intelligent thinking talented consciousness who has dreams of wanting to partake in work that means something to you, while being efficiently compensated enough to survive. You might find you're stuck in a soul crushing job that you head off to day after day simply for the paycheck.

In the film, *Riding in Cars with Boys*, the Drew Barrymore character made a statement in it that forever stuck, *"I still haven't accepted that this is my life. I wish I could be dumb and then I wouldn't know better. And I could be happy and stop hoping."*

The truth was that her character was intelligent, and she was trying to make something with her life, but was constantly struggling against the flow with one roadblock after another. It felt as if she was wasting her time in life. She figured if she wasn't bright, then longing for something greater than what she had, and fighting to make it happen wouldn't be on her radar. She'd be perfectly content working at jobs that didn't matter to her and she wouldn't have to feel miserable spending her days wishing and hoping for a blessing. In the end, she does achieve what she wished and desired for, but it wasn't without the struggle, longing, faith, and action steps taken.

Career transitions are challenging for anyone, because transitions in general are life altering and require effort. Many self-employed entrepreneur success stories also discuss how difficult it can be at first. A Medium friend started out working a day job she hated in New York City. She kept the psychic part of herself quiet at work to avoid ridicule. Reaching the breaking point, she had $10,000 saved and used that to move out to Venice, California. The money quickly left her with the move itself that it resulted in her living out of her car at one point. Eventually, that all turned around with continued faith and prayer. She now has a successful psychic practice and her own home, but it was not without its initial struggles where she almost gave up.

I've been a huge fan of rags to riches success stories since I was a kid. Those are the stories that reveal someone who came from nothing and made something out of their life in the end. They weren't born into money and nor did they have a well to do life. Instead they had to work harder than those who were born into money or had stuff handed to them. They had the endless struggles where it seemed impossible, but they soon climbed the ranks to the top. Those are the inspiring stories that remind you that anyone can do it if they try hard enough.

This isn't necessarily about accumulating financial riches, which is a hollow superficial goal. This is about being able to turn your life purpose, hobby, or passion into a career where you are making enough money that you no longer have to work at jobs you despise just for the paycheck. Rags to riches stories often entail someone who just wanted to be able to do work that was their passion. They weren't looking to make a million dollars. The financial abundance that came flowing in was a positive side effect to them putting effort into their passion. They put in positive energy that came in naturally because they were enjoying the work. This attracted in the financial abundance as a result.

When you feel no guidance or messages coming in from above, then it could be that you're experiencing a block. This is why I often talk about raising your vibration, because doing that begins to dissolve any blocks. One way to raise your vibration is through exercise and working out. I've also forever been a strong advocate for exercise since I was a kid. I've worked out and taken care of myself as much as possible since my teens. I go hiking in the mountains, rock climbing in the desert, and regular jogs and biking on the beach where I'll hang out for hours connecting with Spirit. This is because exercise awakens every cell in your body and soul, but so does being in nature. When you're exercising in nature, then that's a double whammy that assists in raising your vibration. Those cells that are awakened are transporters that communicate with spirit beings from beyond. When those cells awaken, then the information suddenly flows in effortlessly. This is also because exercise does a body good releasing those happy chemical endorphins. Happiness equates to a raised vibration. Couple that with exercising in nature and you transform into a spiritual powerhouse.

When you're happy, your vibration rises, and when you exercise in nature, this releases happy upbeat feelings. Mix the joy with exercising in a nature setting, and you turn into a dynamo. A raised vibration is what acts as a funnel for your Spirit team to communicate with you much more easily. Forcing happiness or pretending to be happy won't work, so it will have to be authentic joy.

Exercise has always been like oxygen to me. The initial getting to the exercise routine may be tough for some, but once you get into some form of cardio to get the body warmed up, then that gets the oxygen working through your cells. It's like soaring above the clouds making you feel good as a result.

FEAR BREEDS HATE

There's nothing more paralyzing than fear. Fear blocks you from moving forward and prevents the positive flow of abundance. Fear can come in the disguise of worry, stress, depression, and anger. It will expand negative emotions and create madness depending on the case. For instance, hate crimes against someone who is different than the antagonist generally begins to breed in the womb of fear. The antagonist might respond by saying, "I'm not afraid of them. I just don't like them." Basically, they don't like anyone that falls into a particular demographic.

Dive down deep as to why you don't like someone. Hating an entire group isn't valid because there are good and bad people in all groups. When you pull one person out of that group you despise and you're locked in a room with them to have a conversation, there is a greater chance that when you both leave that room you'll like them, or you will at least have a bit more compassion, respect, and understanding of them. The only way that will never work is if someone's consciousness is not raised. A limited consciousness permanently resides in darkness unable to break free. The darkness is where fear lives.

I've conducted social experiments where I've placed two people in a room together who are in opposition on the political spectrum. The intention of putting them in the room together was to get them to have friendly conversation outside of their personal political choices. Nine times out of ten they generally ended up liking each other or at least respecting each other despite their personal political values. When you take the time to get to know someone who is different from you, then eventually you come to a greater more compassionate understanding of that person.

You've likely witnessed people endlessly attacking another person over their personal views. This does nothing to change that person. Seeking to understand them and have a cordial sit down conversation with them is more likely to gain some measure of respect. This is not always the case amongst those rare exceptions, but in many paradigms it is. If you already know they can't be reasoned with, then walk away. Someone who puts up resistance has a wall around them that cannot be penetrated by an opposing view. They are not in a position to be receptive to what someone else has to say if it's not aligned with their personal values.

Fear lives within the darkness of ego where it is most at home. Fear is responsible for the chaos energy that forever surrounds the planet when humankind is operating from a low vibration. Fear will make you doubt yourself or it will create a rise in worry energy. Doubts and worry that you will achieve what you desire stems from fear. When that happens, then you need a healthy dose of inspiration that can be found in empowering music, books, or films. This is one of the positives of entertainment, which was created to help people forget about their troubles, help them to lighten up, and give them a dose of inspiration. Balanced entertainers who remain neutral on their personal values while in the public eye don't always get enough credit for this goal at times.

Watch movies about those who came from nothing and made something with their life. Rags to riches stories can be incredibly inspiring. People that had nothing and struggled with little to no money, but soon overcame that and made something with their life. They might be films like *Erin Brockovich, People Vs. Larry Flynt,* or *Joy.*

Many successful known entertainers admit to having self-doubts or fear, which humanizes them and helps them be relatable to their audience. They fear they're not that good or that they'll be found out that they're no good. Of course that isn't true, they are good at what they do, and they are popular, and at the top of their game, but they're also human and have human emotions that their success is a fluke.

It helps to have some perspective that everyone experiences doubts or worries, but don't let that cripple you to the point of non-movement. You rise above it and keep forging forward making the most of what you can do while you are here. You may as well try, because what else do you have to lose?

It took me a long time to move away from relying on regular day jobs to pay me and realize the income was ultimately coming from God. You could do your life purpose work if the financial support part of it is given to God to pay you. You develop less worry and guilt, while gaining more faith and optimism knowing that you're taken care of when you modify your thinking process. This is by changing your perspective to understand that God is ultimately your source of income. This is rather than heavily focusing on a company or a boss to rely on to stay afloat and be taken care of. It takes a great leap of faith to be able to let go of that control. Jobs come and go, but God is always constant. Your reality is, "That's all great, but the checks are written to me by the company I work for. They don't say God on them as the payee." Except, ultimately all forms of abundance are trickling down from God, to the company, and to you. It's no accident that you're at a particular job.

If fear or worry enters your mind, then alter the sentence to something positive, *"God, thank you so much for your help with this. Thank you for the blessings you've bestowed on me to date. Thank you also for ensuring I have a place to live without fear or worry that my bills won't get paid. Thank you for my strong health and happiness."*

A huge lift inside can be felt when changing your sentences from something challenging and negative to something aligned with gratitude, optimism, and faith. When you heavily complain about things never going your way, this creates a huge heavy burden on your soul.

Worry creates more worry, while joy creates more joy. When you feel like your job is not going as planned or you really hate it, and your mind constantly goes there whenever you have a free minute, then take a step back and halt the tone of that thinking. Shift those words to ones of gratitude. Think of the good things you have in your life. The ones that would make your life worse if you didn't have those good things. They can be items such as your car that is in good condition helping you get to and from work without worry. You don't worry much about your car until something goes wrong with it, then you realize how grateful you are to have a car that runs. Don't wait for something bad to happen to realize what you have, but be grateful now. It's easy to take things for granted until those things are taken away. When you are in a negative challenging place, then stop for a moment and direct your attention to those things you do have.

Maybe you've reached the point of feeling sorry for yourself. You say things like, "Why does everyone else get the good stuff, but I'm still struggling to get my share of the blessings?"

The same ones feeling sorry for themselves regularly will also moan about not having any friends. When you look closer, you notice they seem to be surrounded by numerous people who fit the description of a friend. They're still unhappy and despondent not seeing it because perhaps they have conditions on what they expect from a friend. You can have a pity party begging for attention from others, or you can get over it and continue fighting on doing what you're called to do. Never beg for friendship and attention.

One of the general meanings of the Four of Cups card in the Tarot will at times reveal someone feeling sorry for themselves. It seems as if what they want will never come. They sit next to one cup tipped over with their head down disappointed. The card symbolism also shows three cups filled with blessings behind that person, but they're not seeing those gifts.

NOTICING DIVINELY GUIDED ASSISTANCE

Signs and symbols of angelic help are all around when you take the time to notice and pay attention. The first step is to ask for help, since no being in Heaven can intervene or offer assistance for anyone who doesn't ask for help. Some people may not believe that's possible, or they have stopped believing, so they continue to suffer in silence. It doesn't take much effort or time out of your day to stop what you're doing and ask for assistance from above. What do you have to lose by asking? If nothing else you've tried has helped, then what could it hurt to say the words?

The next step is beyond asking for help, but then being aware and paying attention to the repetitive action steps you may be guided to do. You might say, "I asked for help and heard nothing."

Sometimes you're not going to hear the answer through a voice, but you could be given the answer through nudges, signs, taps, symbols, or other ways that could get your attention. Perhaps after you've asked for help, you're invited to an event, but choose not to go because you're uncomfortable with social settings. You failed to notice the synchronicity that took place following you asking for heavenly guidance. Your Spirit team may have been orchestrating a meeting between you and another person who will be at this event. This other person could end up being someone that is connected to a future job you'll have. If you're single, they might be the next relationship lover. Instead you chose to stay home alone when you were being asked to follow this guidance with an action step.

Asking for help also entails asking another person for help. You might be afraid to ask someone for assistance because you're either shy, don't want to bother or burden them, or you have too much pride and are used to doing things yourself. Even the most self-sufficient person can use a hand occasionally. Sometimes the support can come in the form of helpful words of advice from another person. If you're down and out, just talking to someone is a great way to access support.

You might ask for help, but then you start visualizing how you hope the answer will come. You wonder how it will come about, but the visualizing soon forms into worry, which is a prayer killer. When you ask for help, step out of the way and let it come into your life the way it's supposed to and on Divine timing. This is the same way you ask another person for help, but then you end up getting frustrated and taking over to do it yourself, instead of allowing and trusting the other person to handle it in their own way.

Another issue can be feeling guilt about achieving success. You see other successful people and the lower self part of you interjects and brings you down, "I'm nothing like them. Look at this woman, she's so good looking and this is why everyone is buying her products. And look at me, I don't have that look that people are attracted to."

Everyone has something of value to offer the public that helps them in some way. Looks will only get someone so far. Eventually looks fade, so if they don't have something else going for them, then they'll end up being a flash in the pan.

You can see how that negativity can prevent and block you from achieving. Every soul is deserving of good on the planet, and every single person has something positive to offer. In spiritual truth, no one is more special than anyone else. No one is below or above another because in the end all souls are equal, whether it feels like that or not.

In Heaven, all souls are one and this is the same on Earth, even though the ego convinces you that you're either worse or better than another. You are just as deserving of blessings, abundance, and success as any other soul being. There is enough room on the planet for every single soul to experience success. There is always enough to go around. Everyone does and says things in their own way.

You go to a spiritual empowerment event to listen to five different guest speakers on motivation. They are all enjoyable and talking about the same goal and content.

They're each discussing it in their own way. This indicates how everyone has something to offer surrounding the same topic, because not everyone articulates things in the same manner. One speaker might not interest you, but they will interest someone else. There is enough room for everyone to contribute in their own authentic and original way.

In today's world post technology, many have been moving into starting up their own successful self-employment business. There was this motivational YouTube video of this 18-year-old guy who was selling enough product online that he could do that full time. He explained that he doesn't have to take a full time 8-6 corporate office day job that he'll end up despising because he does so well with this internet business. Sometimes he walks along the beach on a Tuesday afternoon when no one is there because they're all at their crushing corporate day jobs. He loves that freedom of space to clear his mind without the crowds. He's able to do that because he sets his own hours and makes enough where he can afford to do that. He's not a millionaire or rich by any means, but he makes enough consistently and regularly to pay his rent and bills without worry. It gives him the luxury of working when he wants to, rather than the rigid inflexible 9a-6p schedule that is the current norm. He gets more done in little time than it takes someone else in a corporate job, and he controls when he chooses to work.

This isn't to knock anyone who enjoys those 8-6 corporate-like soul crushing jobs, but I've never met anyone with that kind of job who has told me they love it, and I converse with a great deal of people. If there were more people than not who loved that kind of a job, then my Spirit team would not have had me write a book like this. I'm out there in the trenches living it, experiencing it, researching it, talking to others who are in it and there's a common theme going on.

Many are interested in more flexible work schedules, where they get more done in a shorter amount of time, and still have some measure of a personal life. They don't want to continue working a soul-crushing job where they find their life has turned into one that consists of living for the weekend. They want to do work that is meaningful to them without feeling overworked and miserable.

While there are many people moving into successful self-employment businesses today more than ever before, they started out by supplementing their income by taking a day job. You just want to do your best to look for a day job that makes you smile enough to not feel stressed and worried, because that energy will carry over to the side hobby you've been working at building. There is the reality that you may not have a choice and will have to accept any day job that comes your way. This is part of the physical survival. You have to take what you need to take to stay afloat and have less worry.

During my day job tenure, I accepted any old job that I wasn't all that happy with, but they did give me some measure of flexibility. It was close to home and offered the safety net of having a job. This enabled me to find an even better job that I truly wanted six months later.

When you feel worry and stress over your day job, or not having enough money to work at your life purpose, then you risk moving into complaining territory. Complaining is an abundance killer. If you spend your life complaining, you will guarantee that you will be given more to complain about.

Several of my friends and I have a pact where we step in if we see someone falling into perpetual complaining. It's pointed out to help them stop. This doesn't mean ignoring a problem one is experiencing, but taking a step back to evaluate what can be done about the issue that is causing the person to complain for days, weeks, and sometimes months.

When you are fearful about not finding a job, it will cause you to vent and complain about that. This isn't telling you to suppress your worries and fears, but rather get to the level of realizing when it's happening. Have your quick complaint about it, but then shift that into something positive like an action step.

CHAPTER FIFTEEN

Become Your Own Authority

A guru in India sat on a stage and talked to an audience about someone who was stressed out at their job.

The guru's response was, "Okay, I hope that you get fired from your job."

The guy said, "Oh no, I don't want to get fired."

The guru explained, "You have a job and you're stressed, so I offer to take the job away from you, but now you're stressed about not having a job. It's all in your mind."

Everyone applauds.

How deep would the guru be in the practical world where he would have to hold a 9-6 job for years with all of the demands that are placed on his back, and all that it entails on his well-being. One reader said that it was easy to wear flowing clothes and sit on a chair on a stage with a turban and dish that out. It's another thing to preach on matters you truly understand because you had to live it and be immersed in it for a long period of time. I take into account all sides to have a greater understanding of the physical reality that different people experience.

On the flip side to counter that, the guru had a point, where yes to an extent the misery is in your mind. When you change your perspective to see that not having that job would be far worse than having it, then you lighten up about it and you shift your perspective on it.

Others may preach about what you need to do, but they may not have lived the kind of life you're undergoing. These can be social media mentors, gurus, or motivational speakers who don't understand why the rest of the world is going through what it's going through. They may not have had to work regular jobs they despise for decades unable to break free. They might not have had to endure child abuse or hardcore addictions. Instead they might have got lucky early on with their self-improvement business. This is intended to illustrate that sometimes you may be drawn to someone informing you about changing your circumstances, but they have not lived through enough turmoil and darkness to understand the nature of rising above it. It can leave you feeling even more confused and dejected unable to grasp why you're not moving out of a situation you feel stuck in.

Someone told me about a popular speaker lecturing the crowd on getting happy, but they added, "That's easy for her to say, she lives in a $10 million dollar mansion and doesn't have to work a job she can't stand just to survive." That comment made me ponder on a deeper level growing more aware and observant about each individual's life history.

When you're battling with something you have trouble

overcoming, you want to hear from someone who lived it rather than some medical doctor who never experienced it. Perhaps the person discussing it has empathy and understanding, or they might have strong psychic spiritual connections that can help, while other times they might have both. If you're seeking healing assistance or motivation, then you'll gravitate towards those that resonate strongly for you. In the end, the intention of all motivators is to motivate you, and if it motivates you to positively change regardless of what that instructor has been through, then they did their job.

As for this particular speaker, she indeed endured a heck of a great deal of trials and tribulations from child sexual abuse to working jobs that sucked out her life force. She had also put off the Divine wisdom that was guiding her to make a big change. When she finally did take that step she catapulted to the top of the charts.

Many well-known spiritual and empowerment related speakers and counselors have moved into the role of encouraging people to be optimistic this lifetime. They do an exceptional job reaching an enormous amount people by inspiring and helping them to initiate action that can lead them closer to achieving bliss, growth, and abundance. Every single person on the planet seeking assistance is not drawn to the same teacher or speaker, which is why it's necessary to have a large selection of teachers in this role. One teacher may work for one person, but not for another. They are aligned with communicating in a language or manner that translates best for you.

If you're new to improving your life, then you know when someone's work has assisted you in positively changing it for the better. Some students are inspired to make healthy life changes, some constantly struggle with it, while others give up. A financially successful motivational speaker who encourages you to be optimistic can be an exceptional motivator. What others have said they take into consideration are two additional major factors associated with a great motivator. One of them is the speaker is financially successful and working for themselves. They have enough income where they work from home full time or wherever they choose. They don't have to slum it day after day forty plus hours a week sitting in traffic to get to and from a job they don't care about that is ultimately killing off their life force. It is easier for someone to tell you to get happy when that's the life they already have. How many people struggling in life will be able to tell others to get happy at that point? The energy discord between both is wide and takes some effort to put into practice. Don't beat yourself up when you experience those periods of frustration, despondence, and pessimism. Be aware of those feelings, make your peace with them, then begin the process of lifting your spirit back into inspiration and optimism.

Many employees work in harsh or toxic environments that do not promote positive morale or a flexible schedule that allows for abundant productivity. Some are working with a toxic colleague or more, or they are working for a superior that fits that mold. What's worse than that is if they work for both a toxic boss and a toxic colleague. The vibrational distance between being in that space compared to achieving what a financially successful motivating teacher has is super wide to overcome. It is not impossible to do when you see that someone else was able to make that leap and transition. Knowing your motivator was able to do that is an excellent motivation to have in itself.

The financially successful teacher has the life that others dream of, so therefore it's easier for them to be optimistic. They no longer have the restrictions that prohibit them from achieving easy bliss. They're no longer walking in the shoes of someone working a job they despise that is killing off their life force and preventing them from remaining optimistic. We're they this optimistic when they had to slum it in a job they despised in a crummy apartment? It was more than likely a huge struggle for them to get positive around the clock in that instant than it is now doing work they love. Even the most wonderful upbeat positive teacher will have some down feeling days too, but you're not seeing that on camera.

The other factor is that some speakers have a naturally sunny disposition. They could have been born bubbly, bouncy, and extroverted with fewer horrid experiences to overcome. These are things such as they're not battling with mental, emotional, or physical disorders, or addictions and abuse that make it challenging everyday to have that award winning bright personality that takes people by storm when they enter a room.

It's challenging to get someone suffering from daily anxiety or depression to shift that energy when they have what some might call a chemical imbalance. Maybe you consume substances that are not great for you thus altering your state of mind to something worse. You take those substances because it gives you a temporary high. Soon that high wears off and you're miserable again until you consume the substance again. This is in order to keep going.

It's easy to sell positive thinking when you're a million-dollar speaker or you work for yourself. I'm sure you would love to meet the 9-6 Monday thru Friday employee who works a job they don't care about for a paycheck and simultaneously pushes perpetual positive thinking. They are rare and some companies are lucky to have that one person in there that brings joy just by being a part of that staff.

Spiritual teachers, speakers, and motivators assist in guiding you in a more enlightened direction, but ultimately you are your own authority. You have the true answers within as to what changes you need to make for yourself to get happy.

I grew up being physically, mentally, spiritually, and emotionally abused by one of my parents. It was repetitive and severe enough that my soul consciousness broke and split apart into numerous selves. I ended up struggling through alcohol, drug, and pill addictions, which also transferred into broken relationships. While things are much better and at peace today than back then, I still struggle to forge forward battling the side effects it brought on at times.

Growing up, I wanted to hear from someone who is or has had to drudge it day after day for decades and eventually escaped that to do what they love full time. Or they were still able to be endlessly optimistic and naturally motivated while working that kind of job. I have never in all my years in the work force encountered someone who was permanently optimistic. Most of them appeared miserable or disappointed in their life.

There are a great many teachers, role models, and motivators threaded around the world with past histories that fit the rags to riches scenario. Those were the ones I gravitated towards to see someone rise up from the slums of their life to the one they had only envisioned in dreams of Heaven.

Many people look to motivational speakers to inspire them, give them great life tips, or just to hear positive words, but you create your own life. You choose how it will go. If you don't like your life, then take action steps to change it. You be your own motivator. If you feel that you can't change it, can't move out of the place you live in, can't leave the job you hate for financial reasons, then you will remain in that position until you take steps to change it.

Living for the Weekend

The odds of winning the lottery jackpot are slim to none, so you can't rely on that, but certainly buying a ticket can increase the rare probability of winning. What you can do is take action steps towards making the life you want a reality. Many people have done it. They've worked jobs they've hated and eventually worked jobs they loved or moved into careers working for themselves. Working for yourself where you call the shots can have its drawbacks. You still have to answer to yourself and ensure you have consistent income coming in so you can pay your bills. Prayer and positive affirmations help alter your perception, but it still needs to be coupled with action since it is rare that anything magnificent will land in your lap with no effort. Even just a little effort goes a long way as it gets that energy moving in that direction.

While many will talk about how you have to be happy first and then the abundance will come, it's easy to say that when you have the abundance, therefore it's not always entirely true. The reality is there are many miserable people that achieved financial abundance in their lifetime and we're still miserable afterwards.

Be as optimistic as you can be in general, since no one is rubbed the right way being around a miserable grump, but it certainly won't play that big of a part in preventing what you want from coming to you. People that achieved what they wanted regardless of being miserable or optimistic is because they worked hard and went after it without stopping. It's hard work and persistence that helps you achieve. It's not giving up no matter how many setbacks or roadblocks get in your way.

It's also more than practicing positive thinking and bliss in hopes of achieving the ultimate reward, which are abundance and endless blessings. Don't be mistaken by this message telling you to think negatively instead. By all means, positive thinking is always the way to go, but in the most efficient way. You cannot deny how you're feeling by masking it with false positive thinking in order to convince you that you are positive, when deep down you are miserable. You are miserable with where your life is at, miserable that you don't have a lover, miserable that you're not doing work that you love, miserable that your life is not where you thought it would be, and miserable because you feel perpetually stuck. Those are valid feelings that need to be addressed and dealt with one at a time. You can choose to be miserable for a lifetime that the lover did not come, or you can make the most of it and accept it by letting it go.

The problem with saying that positive thinking is not the way to go is that it confuses one by glorifying negative thinking. It's basically saying, "Hey, it's okay to be miserable. If that's how you feel, then let it out and be proud of that."

That's dangerous to say since people are miserable and negative enough. No one has any problem being negative. It takes work to be positive, but the positive feeling has to be experienced naturally. If it's forced, then it's still negative with a false layer of optimism.

Numerous studies revealed surprising revelations that successful business entrepreneur millionaires were those who had a tough time in school. They might not have gone to College, but might have graduated from High School with a B or C average and sometimes lower. Most were not "A" students with a 4.0 GPA. I remember before my days in the Entertainment Industry that in the 1980's it was known that bigwig producers would make someone with a College Degree serve coffee just to prove that in the end it doesn't matter to them.

This isn't justifying or discrediting school achievers, nor is it attempting to sway anyone from striving to be your best in school. This is illustrating to those who have struggled, not to give up. Don't believe you won't amount to anything because you did poorly in school or didn't receive a degree. There are numerous examples of people who did poorly in school, came from a poor or middle class background, yet ended up becoming millionaires. This is partially because they tried harder, conveyed passion and dedication. They used more mental prowess to succeed despite not having a degree or a high GPA. They were optimistic, persistent, and streets smart.

A top CEO of a well-known real estate franchise informed me that she never went to College, but instead received her degree at the "school of hard knocks". Her offices combined bring in over $150 million in real estate revenue. Not bad for someone who came from nothing, didn't do well in school, and with little education.

Everyone entertains doubts or negative thinking at some point, including the most evolved enlightened being. It is humanely impossible for one person to be 100% positive in thinking every second of their life. Earth is not Heaven, and doubts and negative thinking will creep up even with the most positive appearing person. If you think positive, then you will achieve blessings and rewards. This is not always true and can put someone into a dangerous predicament. The secret to achieving blessings is a combination of factors that include taking action as well as being optimistic that you can do it. You can't layer your negative thoughts with positive thinking. This is like taking a pill to numb emotional pain. It may numb those rough edges, but it doesn't get rid of the issues unless it's addressed and dealt with in order to heal and then release it. Then you have a clean slate to forge forward fearlessly.

CHAPTER SIXTEEN

You Are Worthy
and Deserving of Blessings

It takes a warrior like effort to not allow anything to kill off your life force and prevent you from working on your passion and life purpose. There are a great many rags to riches stories that have been told throughout history. They included people who were once struggling and wondering if they'd ever break free from their self-imprisoned life, but they kept working hard on what they desired on the side during their down time. Eventually, they transitioned out of that and into what they love.

Keep forging on ahead fearlessly and making a personal pact to contribute a little bit of what you love towards your lifelong goals each day for a minimum of thirty minutes to an hour. Whether that hour is used to read and research up on your areas of interest, or you devote positive action steps towards what will ultimately be your life purpose income, such as creating a website, a social media page, postcards, etc. Putting in a tiny bit of time is better than putting in no time.

Become independent and a self-sufficient self-starter that manages your life with enthusiasm and finesse. Working seventy hours a week doesn't mean you're a hard worker. It just means you're lousy at time management. It's a world of workaholics plugging away at meaningless tasks that usually amount to a great deal of nothing in the end. This carries off into all aspects of your life, but is primarily beneficial for those in leadership or supervising positions.

When spreading yourself too thin, you want to ensure to be extra careful about what you're putting into your body. You might complain you're too tired or don't have enough time or energy to contribute up to an hour a day into what could potentially be your full-time job. This is a dilemma and a block for you, but if this is work you truly love, then it doesn't feel like work. It's something you enjoy doing, so working on it is rarely a problem. When someone cheerfully wants to do something, they will do it no matter how tired they are. In fact, putting in work on your passion and love gives you a positive lift, a boost, and raises your vibration. All of which are ingredients in that recipe for attracting in positive circumstances, more energy, and abundance.

Raising your vibration is a crucial element in giving you greater energy and a brighter mood. This encourages you to make the time to contribute towards what you love. After a long laborious and tedious day at work at your day job, you may be sapped off life force energy to keep going after you've left your job. When you have more continuous energy, then that's energy to help push you to contribute towards work that you love, such as your life purpose passion work during those moments when you're not at your day job.

The reason you might be exhausted at the end of each day is not always because work is so tough at your day job, but it's because this job does not excite you on any level. When you experience excitement, then the feel good chemical dopamine is released into your system. When you despise what you do, then this depletes the dopamine chemical, which sucks the life force energy right out of you making you feel tired.

When I'm doing what I love, then the energy keeps going beyond twelve hours where I don't want to stop. It's a perpetual rushed excited high, because I'm doing what I love that it doesn't feel like work. It's fun and I'm getting paid for it too! On top of that, I'm being extra careful with what I put into my body and system. You know that if you have a glass of wine or a beer in the middle of the day, then you're unlikely to put in any work into what you love. Keeping your energy high and motivated on those days that you want to work on your life purpose requires taking care of all aspects of your body, mind, and soul. When you believe that great things will happen for you, then great things will happen! The ingredients in this recipe include having a positive attitude, strong faith, asking for help in prayer, and taking action. Like the Journey song title says, "Don't stop believing."

For some successful people, there will come that point when the floodgates of abundance open and it soars wonderfully into your world. Some personalities will allow the darkness of ego to rise convincing you to panic and worry that it's a fluke and will be taken away from you soon enough. Some form of worry could be considered understandable, but don't let it consume and drown you. Quickly move away from that way of thinking and receive the blessings with a positive spirit.

Whenever I started a new film production for the studios, people were unaware that I had the occasional minor fear briefly in the beginning years. I would worry the first few days that I might get fired. I would go into a serious meditation exercise the night before my first day on the job and be prepared to dive on in and hit the ground running. The minor fear or worry was so miniscule though that it didn't dominate, but was rather a fleeting thought that peeked its face in, then blew away just as quickly. After the first number of days on the gig, the fears would subside, as I'd fall into the groove of the job. Employers would later comment they were surprised to hear that I'd have doubts in the beginning, because it never showed. It would pop in for thirty seconds, then pop right out as I'd re-align, let it go, and just do the best job I can do.

It's a wonderful and awesome thing when circumstances start flowing positively. You think, "Wow, I can't believe how great this is. I hope it doesn't go away and I don't lose it."

Don't doubt, just accept, and enjoy the wave of excitement and optimism. Allow any roadblocks in your life to fall away as you move into smooth calm waters up ahead.

Get optimistic, have faith, and trust in God and your Spirit team. When you're worried about something, then ask and pray for intervention to remove those worries. Make this prayer request daily if the worry continues. Don't give up or try to do it yourself, but turn your worries into prayer, since that's what can help lift the burdens that negative thoughts and feelings can produce.

Prayer is intended to help you move away from worry and fear. You invalidate a prayer when you continue to worry afterwards. The worry tells Spirit that you don't trust their intervention and assistance and so you will continue to worry as a backup plan in case God doesn't come through. When you receive repeated nudges after the prayer to take action on something, then take action.

When circumstances become too great, then take some time out in quiet meditation or contemplation. Create a sanctuary ambiance at home or in your room. Disconnect from people and technology for several hours or even the day, and spend that time conversing with God, a higher power, and the universe. Go on a day or weekend trip with a positive friend, or by yourself if you find that more beneficial.

Let go of feelings of resentment and jealousy about other people who seem to be more successful than you are at this point. This success may be in career, love, or life in general. You find yourself saying things like, "Why does she have him for a boyfriend? I'm so much better than she is, I don't get it."

Or, "I should be way more successful than they are. I work harder and I'm smarter."

You want to avoid falling into that kind of envy energy because that will ensure you stay single or will never be successful. It's understandable to a point that you are feeling frustrated because you are just as deserving as anyone else. Resentment builds and overpowers you and crushes your soul in the process.

The flipside is if you are financially successful, then don't feel guilty about making money in general, or making more money than others. Money is energy, so when you're being paid for services you provide, then that is an exchange of energy. Feel no guilt about making money or how you choose to spend it. You are worthy of making money for any work you do. Don't apologize for being blessed.

Avoid resentment, jealousy, worry, or fear associated with money. Visualize the awesome circumstances you'd be able to partake in due to making enough money. Imagine how many people's lives you'd be able to change and help positively.

Your imagination is a powerful divine instrument of God, so use it to your advantage. You're already spending the day thinking, perhaps thinking about useless chores and tasks, but how about thinking about something good. Pay attention to those ideas that enter your mind. A great deal of it is coming from above. Look at the great music, books, art, and movies over the course of history alone that started out with one person's idea and rapidly expanded to the point where there is a 600-man crew filming it into a visual story. It's awesome what people have been able to create.

The angels don't want to see someone destined for greatness working in a day job that kills off their life force. They are not keeping you down, and nor are they keeping you there to punish you. There could be various reasons as to why you're still there that is beyond your control. They could be working diligently behind the scenes with aligning circumstances that work in your favor to get you to work full time in your self-employed business.

Release any vows of poverty you might have made in a past life, regardless if you believe in past lives or not. It won't hurt you to verbally say, *"I release all vows of poverty I might have made in this life or any previous ones, in all directions of time."*

There are some circumstances, which cannot practically be understood by the human mind. Navigate through life with an open mind and consciousness over what is unseen.

Have no fear or doubts in believing in Heaven, God,

Jesus, and your Spirit team. Believe that you are watched over and are not being ignored, even on those days when you just want to throw in the towel and permanently give up. Don't give up because there is a reason you are here. Spirit can see the good up ahead, even when you feel like this is it.

The world spins around, circumstances change, friendships come and go, some stay, some leave, people pass on, life goes on for the soul. Study and read up on success stories that you can do it! Don't feel resentment or jealousy over someone else's work, but feel inspired and motivated by it instead. It's to help you feel those things so that you can believe that yes you can do it too.

When one thinks of success they automatically equate it to money, but success is not always financial or monetary. The utmost form of success is how evolved your soul develops in one lifetime. Since this is the true measure of Spirit's view of success, then you should thrive to push the billionaire mark. Rise above the world around you and dive deep into the depths of possibilities by working to expand your mind and consciousness. Seek out the vast reservoirs of wisdom, knowledge, and intelligence that the Universe holds. Take that by the reigns and soar full speed ahead today. Make some great things happen in your life now.

Living for the Weekend

ALSO BY KEVIN HUNTER

Warrior of Light
Empowering Spirit Wisdom
Darkness of Ego
Realm of the Wise One
Transcending Utopia
Reaching for the Warrior Within
Spirit Guides and Angels
Soul Mates and Twin Flames
Raising Your Vibration
Divine Messages for Humanity
Connecting with the Archangels
The Seven Deadly Sins
A Beginner's Guide to the Four Psychic Clair Senses
Tarot Card Meanings
Living For the Weekend
Twin Flame Soul Connections
Monsters and Angels
Love Party of One
Ignite Your Inner Life Force
Awaken Your Creative Spirit
The Essential Kevin Hunter Collection

The Essential Kevin Hunter Collection
Available in Paperback and E-book

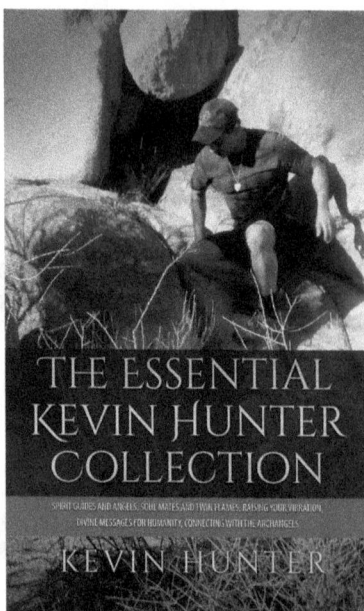

THE ESSENTIAL
KEVIN HUNTER
COLLECTION

Featuring the following books:
Warrior of Light, Empowering Spirit Wisdom, Darkness of Ego,
Spirit Guides and Angels, Soul Mates and Twin Flames, Raising
Your Vibration, Divine Messages for Humanity, and Connecting
with the Archangels.

TRANSCENDING UTOPIA
Reopening the Pathway to Divinity
Available in Paperback and E-book

Transcending Utopia is packed with practical and spirit knowledge that focuses on enhancing your life through empowering divinely guided spiritual related teachings, inspiration, wisdom, guidance, and messages. The way to accelerate existence on Earth towards Utopia is if every person on the planet resided in their soul's true nature, which is in a state of all love, joy, and peace. The ultimate Nirvana is surpassing that perfection through methods that a limited consciousness could ever dream possible. This is the exceptional glory your soul was born into before the dense turbulence of Earthly life enveloped and suffocated you.

Transcending Utopia is to go beyond your limits and travel outside of the generic mundane materialistic achievement that human beings taught one another to thrive for. A utopian society is where everything is perfectly blissful on all levels according to the sanctified values you were born with. The sensations connected to how flawless everything feels in that moment reveals the authentic perfection you were made from. Utopia is the ideal paradise as imagined in one's dreams that seems to be inaccessible by human standards. It is a state of mind that is possible to reach by adopting broader ways of looking at circumstances while being disciplined about how you conduct your life. You search for a sign of this utopia through external means, only to be consistently left with disappointment. This is because utopia begins and ends inside the spark that burns within your spirit like a pilot light waiting to be ignited.

WARRIOR OF LIGHT
Messages from my Guides and Angels

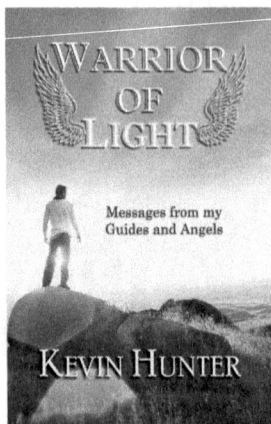

There are legions of angels, spirit guides, and departed loved ones in heaven that watch and guide you on your journey here on Earth. They are around to make your life easier and less stressful. Do you pay attention to the nudges, guidance, and messages given to you? There are many who live lives full of negativity and stress while trying to make ends meet. This can shake your faith as it leads you down paths of addictions, unhealthy life choices, and negative relationship connections. Learn how you can recognize the guidance of your own Spirit team of guides and angels around you. Author, Kevin Hunter, relays heavenly guided messages about getting humanity, the world, and yourself into shape. He delivers the guidance passed onto him by his own Spirit team on how to fine tune your body, soul and raise your vibration. Doing this can help you gain hope and faith in your own life in order to start attracting in more abundance.

EMPOWERING SPIRIT WISDOM
A Warrior of Light's Guide on Love, Career and the Spirit World

Kevin Hunter relays heavenly, guided messages for everyday life concerns with his book, *Empowering Spirit Wisdom*. Some of the topics covered are your soul, spirit and the power of the light, laws of attraction, finding meaningful work, transforming your professional and personal life, navigating through the various stages of dating and love relationships, as well as other practical affirmations and messages from the Archangels. Kevin Hunter passes on the sensible wisdom given to him by his own Spirit team in this inspirational book.

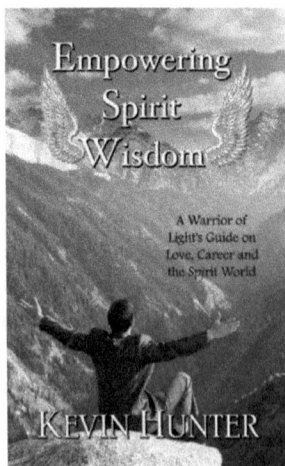

176

DARKNESS OF EGO

In *Darkness of Ego*, author Kevin Hunter infuses some of the guidance, messages, and wisdom he's received from his Spirit team surrounding all things ego related. The ego is one of the most damaging culprits in human life. Therefore, it is essential to understand the nature of the beast in order to navigate gracefully out of it when it spins out of control. Some of the topics covered in *Darkness of Ego* are humanity's destruction, mass hysteria, karmic debt, and the power of the mind, heaven's gate, the ego's war on love and relationships, and much more.

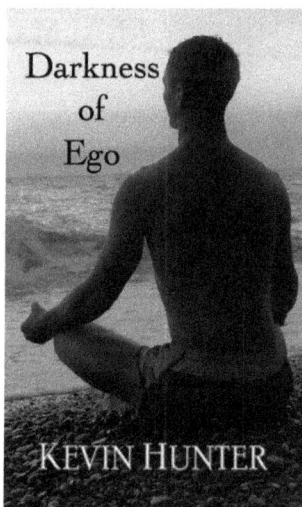

REACHING FOR THE WARRIOR WITHIN

Reaching for the Warrior Within is the author's personal story recounting a volatile childhood. This led him to a path of addictions, anxiety and overindulgence in alcohol, drugs, cigarettes and destructive relationships. As a survival mechanism, he split into many different "selves". He credits turning his life around, not by therapy, but by simultaneously paying attention to the messages he has been receiving from his Spirit team in Heaven since birth.

KEVIN HUNTER

REALM OF THE WISE ONE

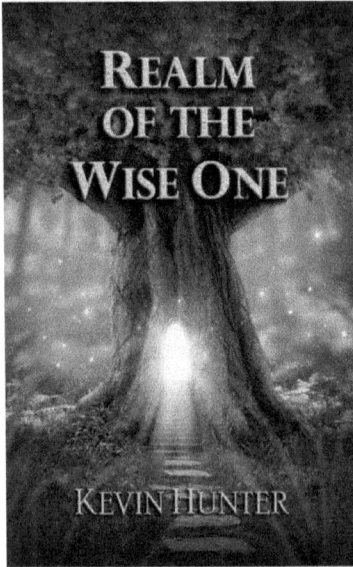

In the Spirit Worlds and the dimensions that exist, reside numerous kingdoms that house a plethora of Spirits that inhabit various forms. One of these tribes is called the Wise Ones, a darker breed in the spirit realm who often chooses to incarnate into a human body one lifetime after another for important purposes.

The *Realm of the Wise One* takes you on a magical journey to the spirit world where the Wise Ones dwell. This is followed with in-depth and detailed information on how to recognize a human soul who has incarnated from the Wise One Realm. Author, Kevin Hunter, is a Wise One who uses the knowledge passed onto him by his Spirit team of Guides and Angels to relay the wisdom surrounding all things Wise One. He discusses the traits, purposes, gifts, roles, and personalities among other things that make up someone who is a Wise One. Wise Ones have come in the guises of teachers, shaman, leaders, hunters, mediums, entertainers and others. *Realm of the Wise One* is an informational guide devoted to the tribe of the Wise Ones, both in human form and on the other side.

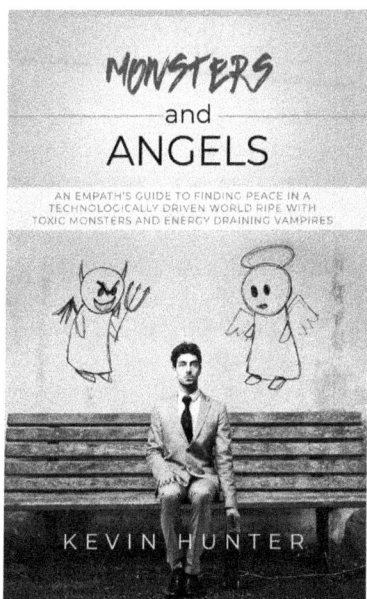

MONSTERS AND ANGELS

*An Empath's Guide to Finding Peace
in a Technologically Driven World
Ripe with Toxic Monsters and
Energy Draining Vampires*

Every person on the planet is capable of being empathic and sensitive, to becoming an energy vampire or toxic monster. No one is exempt from displaying the darker sides of their ego. The easiest and most efficient way to spread any kind of energy is online. Every time you log onto the Internet, there is a larger chance you're going to see something related to the news, media, or gossip areas thrown in front of you, even if you attempt to avoid it as much as possible. You're absorbing everything that your consciousness faces, including the ugly and the wicked, which has its own consequences. This tempestuous energy is tossed into the Universe ultimately creating a flame-throwing battleground inside and around you.

Monsters and Angels discusses how technology, media, and social media have an immense power in distributing both positive and negative influences far and wide. This is about being mindful of what can negatively affect your state of being, and how to counter and avoid that when and wherever possible. This is why it's beneficial to govern yourself, your life, and your surroundings like a strict disciplined executive.

Some of the topics discussed include: *Energy vampires, toxic monsters, sensitive angels, and empaths, the technological craze, being sensitive in a technical driven world, connecting through technical means, the insanity of the ego, steering clear of drama, finding balance in the media, technological detox tips, rising above the mundane and into the Divine, climbing beyond superficiality, and centering your inner light.*

IGNITE YOUR INNER LIFE FORCE

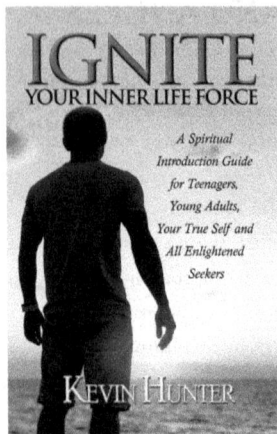

Ignite Your Inner Life Force is an introduction guide for teens, young adults, and anyone seeking answers, messages, and guidance and surrounding spiritual empowerment. This is from understanding what Heaven, the soul, and spiritual beings are to knowing when you are connecting with your Spirit team of Guides and Angels. Some of the topics covered are communicating with Heaven, working with your Spirit team, what your higher self is, your life purpose and soul contract, what the ego is, love and relationships, your vibration energy, shifting your consciousness and thinking for yourself even when you stand alone. This is an in-depth primer manual offering you foundation as you find a higher purpose navigating through your personal journey in today's modern day practical world.

AWAKEN YOUR CREATIVE SPIRIT

Your creative spirit is more than being artistic and getting involved in creativity pursuits, although this is a good part of it. When your creative spirit is activated by a high vibration state of being, then this is the space you create from. You can apply this to your dealings in life, your creative and artistic pursuits, and to having a greater communication line with your Spirit team on the Other Side. *Awaken Your Creative Spirit* is an overview of what it means to have access to Divine assistance and how that plays a part in arousing the muse within you in order to bring your state of mind into a happier space.

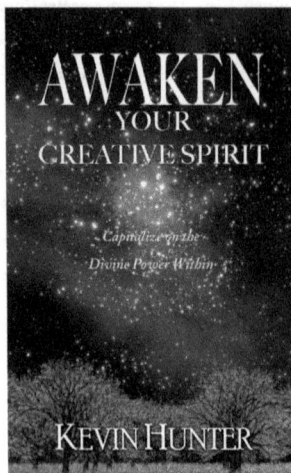

The *Warrior of Light* series of pocket books are available in paperback and E-book called, *Spirit Guides and Angels, Soul Mates and Twin Flames, Divine Messages for Humanity, Raising Your Vibration, Connecting with the Archangels*, and *The Seven Deadly Sins*

TAROT CARD MEANINGS

A Beginner's Guide to the
FOUR PSYCHIC CLAIR SENSES

Learn about the four main psychic clair senses to help you connect with Heaven, the Spirit World, and the Other Side. Take that one step further and use those senses to read the Tarot! *Tarot Card Meanings* is an encyclopedia reference guide that takes the Tarot apprentice reader through each of the 78 Tarot Cards offering the potential general meanings and interpretations that could be applied when conducting a reading, whether it be spiritual, love, general, or work related questions. This is an easy to understand manual for the Tarot novice that is having trouble interpreting cards for themselves, or a Tarot reader who loves the craft and is looking for a refresher or another point of view. The *Four Psychic Clair Senses* focuses on the main channels that Heaven and Spirit communicate with you. *Both books are available in Paperback and E-book wherever books are sold.*

About Kevin Hunter

Kevin Hunter is an author, love expert, and channeler. His books tackle a variety of genres and tend to have a strong male protagonist. The messages and themes he weaves in his work surround Spirit's own communications of love and respect, which he channels and infuses into his writing work.

His spiritually based empowerment books include *Warrior of Light, Empowering Spirit Wisdom, Realm of the Wise One, Reaching for the Warrior Within, Darkness of Ego, Transcending Utopia, Living for the Weekend, Ignite Your Inner Life Force, Awaken Your Creative Spirit,* and *Tarot Card Meanings.* His metaphysical pocket books series include, *Spirit Guides and Angels, Soul Mates and Twin Flames, Raising Your Vibration, Divine Messages for Humanity, Connecting with the Archangels, Four Psychic Clair Senses, Twin Flame Soul Connections, The Seven Deadly Sins,* and *Monsters and Angels.* He is also the author of the dating singles guide *Love Party of One,* the horror/drama, *Paint the Silence,* and the modern day erotic love story, *Jagger's Revolution.*

Before becoming an author, Kevin started out in the entertainment business in 1996 as the personal development guy to one of Hollywood's most respected talent, Michelle Pfeiffer, for her boutique production company, Via Rosa Productions. She dissolved her company after several years and he made a move into coordinating film productions for the studios on such films as *One Fine Day, A Thousand Acres, The Deep End of the Ocean, Crazy in Alabama, The Perfect Storm, Original Sin, Harry Potter & the Sorcerer's Stone, Dr. Dolittle 2,* and *Carolina.* He considers himself a beach bum born and raised in Southern California. For more information, www.kevin-hunter.com